BRIDGWATER
St. Matthew
FAIR

GUY BELSHAW

St. Matthew's Fair, has been held in Bridgwater since 1249, opening traditionally on the last Wednesday in September, lasting for four days, ending on the Saturday.

Originally a sheep Fair, it is also an event when the Romanies bring their ponies to be sold privately at the site. It is St Matthew's Field where most people seek entertainment at the largest fun fair in the West. From the traditional roundabout to the latest white-knuckle thrill ride, Bridgwater Fair is one of the most important dates in the travelling showman's calendar.

Local fairground historian and *World's Fair* correspondent, Guy Belshaw, looks into the fair's past and, using photographs from a number of sources, many previously unpublished, illustrates the history of St. Matthew's Fair.

New Era Publications

Published by:
New Era Publications
P.O. Box 549
Tweedale
Telford
TF7 5WA

ISBN 0 9535097 5 3

Printed by RCS plc
Randall Park Way
Retford DN22 7WF

New Era Publications

Introduction

Above: West Street Market in the 1950s. *[Rod Fitzhugh]*

Bridgwater's St Matthew's Fair can trace its origins back to 1249 with a fair on St. Matthew's Day, September 21st, for eight days. This is the direct ancestor of the event that survives to this day. King John granted the town three charters in 1200, the third of which dealt with the rights to hold markets and fairs.

The Fair, according to references dated 1379, was already well established and very profitable by the fourteenth century, and has for hundreds of years been held on St .Matthew's Field outside the West Gate of the town. This is clearly proved by a conveyance of 1404 which transfers a burgage whose position is described as "outside the West Gate of the town of Bridgwater as it were on the way to St. Matthews Fair".

Initially held in the centre of the town, the fair became so large and disrupted the everyday business of the town that in 1404 it was moved out to the countryside beyond the West Gate of the town, the site of which is now the West Street area. Historically, both religious and economic significance attaches to the fair. St Matthew's Fair has a rich and colourful history and what is now a pleasure fair and street market grew out of centuries of

being merely an added attraction to the main business of the buying and selling of livestock.

What distinguishes Bridgwater from the other great pleasure fairs, such as Nottingham Goose Fair and Hull Fair, is that it has been held on the same site for centuries. St Matthew's survives as a fair where livestock is traded and it was only the blight of foot and mouth disease in 2001 that ended the famous sheep sales. No break occurred during the hostilities of either of the two world wars.

The Fair which was primarily for the sale of livestock and the produce of the fertile Somerset agricultural plain as well as a place that attracted itinerant entertainers. Peddlers and hawkers would have come to sell their wares. Somerset's market towns, had charters conferred on them in profusion in the twelfth and thirteenth centuries but it was Bridgwater's St. Matthew's Fair which grew to become the largest and most famous in the West Country. Always held on the last Wednesday in September it has, for the past 600 years, always been held on the site of the old West Gate, and St Matthews's Field.

Above: The sheep auction.

The date of the last Wednesday in September was fixed in 1857 when it was altered from 2nd October. The change of date had little impact on business. The *Bridgwater Times* noted that: *"The number of beasts in the field did not exceed 400."*

Bridgwater was an important trading town, not only as a market centre for the surrounding countryside, but from the 15th century served as a vital inland port and had important trading links with Ireland, France, Spain, Italy, the Baltic and Scandinavia, Russia, Canada and the East Indies. The main export was the famous cloth produced in the town and at other places in Somerset.

From the eighteenth century the brick and roofing tile industry began and flourished for the next two centuries. Coastal shipping took these products, for which the town became famous, to ports in Wales and around the British Isles.

It was its position as a thriving port that gave the town its distinct character. Quite apart from its sleepy Somerset neighbours, Bridgwater was always more than a market town. The river Parrett dominates the town and brought ships carrying wines and spirits from France, Spain Italy and Barbados, timber and furs from Scandinavia and goods such as hides, cider, grain, and livestock as well as the important cloth were exported. This brisk import and export trade from the Middle Ages up until the Second World War lent a cosmopolitan flavour to the town.

The use of larger ships coupled with the difficult tides and currents led to a decline in the use of the docks which closed to commercial shipping in 1971, although the port of Bridgwater still operates from Dunball.

From the port grew a diverse industrial town, bricks and tiles were produced in large quantity from the early 18th century and dominated manufacturing industry of the town for the next two centuries and the clay pits and brick kilns were a familiar sight. The industrial revolution and the coming of the railways expanded the town's manufacturing industries and brought about further development.

As well as becoming Somerset's most industrialised town, at its heart was the market, a trading centre for a cornucopia of produce from the rich agricultural land that surrounds the town. Dairy products from the lush pastures of the Somerset levels and the valley of the Parrett from Burrowbridge to Combwich. Cheese from the Mendips, basketware made from withies grown on the levels, apples and cider from the Orchards, plentiful in every village and fish and elvers from the river and the nearby Bristol Channel.

High on the nearby Quantock hills sheep of excellent quality were produced and once a year the ponies were driven down from the hills to be sold at St Matthew's Fair. The ponies were held at such villages as Nether Stowey, which lies at the foot of the Quantocks to be watered and sorted prior to being driven in to the fair.

The sheep and pony sales gave the fair its character. A great annual gathering for all those who earned their living from the land and maybe met only once a year at Bridgwater Fair. The Romany gypsy, although a distinctly different ethnic and social group to fairground travellers, has long been associated with the fair. Trading in horse and ponies remains a popular element of the fair into the 21st century. The fair also acted as a

Above and below: Cattle sales in the early years of the 20th Century. Behind the pens are the shows of Messrs. Hancock and Anderton & Rowland, and the beer tents, one of which was for the 'labouring classes' whilst the other served the better off visitors to the fair. *[Rod Fitzhugh]*

hiring fair up until the first decade of the 20th century; a formal opportunity for tradesman and servants to offer themselves for hire for the next year.

In the 19th century the Thursday of the fair was known as "servant's day" for shop assistants and Friday night was for factory workers and domestic servants. In the first half of the 20th century, Wednesday was farmer's day, Thursday was tradesman's. The other great tradition of the fair is the street market in West Street.

At one time the street of small terraced houses with numerous courts was lined with booths licensed for the sale of intoxicating liquor and many of the houses in the street were also licensed.

West Street was the site of the town's weekly sheep market and the street was host to both sheep and market goods before the Second World War, when sheep sales were transferred to St Matthews's Field.

In the photo of the sheep penned in ready for auction (below) you can notice the street's sloping sides. West Street and surrounding area was the site of narrow Victorian courts. Along with the terraces the whole of West Street was demolished in 1964 and replaced with the tower block and the modern development of three-storey flats and businesses.

The market draws huge crowds and the commodities on sale, with a few exceptions, have not changed much since this report in the *Market Trader* newspaper in 1938: *"A popular feature of the street market is the auctioneers of china, ornaments and other household goods. The china goods stalls seemed larger and more colourful .The vendors of china and plaster ornaments had bigger spreads than I had ever seen before. Clothing salesmen seemed to be in greater strength, some of them pitching in the cattle market.*

Demonstrators were few, though I must compliment on his style the cockney "dem" working metal and wood polish. Rock, Panam (sweets) and edibles began with Percy Huish's stall at the bottom of the street and finished at the top with nougat and chocolates. Fruit salesman had a hard time apart from one in the gate with baskets of first class stuff which was disposed of in a four handed pitched by means of the wheel and tickets. An innovation was an RAF recruiting van complete with loud speakers. There were a few Escape artistes and a couple of second sight readers."

Local people offering fruit vegetables, eggs poultry and game and home produced preserves were a familiar sight before the Second World War. The rents are now high by street market standards and only professional traders take space, although charity stands and the Salvation Army are all permitted their customary places.

A somewhat less regulated market of sorts exists beyond the fair in the area of the former livestock sale area where goods aimed specifically at the travelling

Below: Sheep pens in West Street. *[Rod Fitzhugh]*

Above: China and glass salesman on West Street in the 1950s. *[Lionel Bathe, courtesy of the National Fairground Archive]*

showfolk are offered for sale alongside more traditional market goods such and toys and clothes.

At the start of the 21st century the market remains as buoyant lively and popular as ever a traditional mix of cut price textiles, garden bulbs, fast food, confectionery, palmists, demonstrators of kitchen gadgets and of course the type of china pitchers reported upon in 1938.

Horses and ponies have been traded at the fair since records began. In the 19th century and well in to the 20th there was a strong contingent of Irish horse traders present at the fair offering Irish colts and buying stock. The close proximity of the Exmoor and Quantock pony herd has made St. Matthew's a convenient fair to buy and sell 20th century Ponies. The distinctive breeds of Exmoor and Quantock ponies were much in demand up until the Second World War. The Exmoor is a very distinctive breed with whitish colouring around the muzzle and wide chest .It is the oldest and purist of the British native pony breeds. Natural selection has designed a pony suited to survival in the cold wet Exmoor climate.

The herds of Ponies found on the Quantocks are of mixed breed although the two share common characteristics of being able to survive without food or shelter from man. The Exmoor is sought after for many equine businesses such as riding schools and trekking. The pure Exmoor was a valuable commodity and good examples of the breed regularly sold for between £30

and £40 in the 1860's. Draught horses or 'Cart Colts' were another sought after commodity.

Bridgwater was only one of a whole number of fairs dealing in horses, cattle and sheep during late September and early October in the 19th century. The big Gloucester Barton Fair often fell on the same day and the smaller but well supported Wiveliscombe Fair was usually held the same week. Westonzoyland a few miles away held a large fair on September 8th by virtue of a royal charter as did Langport and Yeovil; even small villages such as Broomfield had its own fair.

Glastonbury Tor Fair was a large autumn event which was a livestock mart as well a very large pleasure this event, despite its rich history was a casualty of the redevelopment of the field were for hundreds of years it had been held. The showman were offered an alternative site, but the removal from the traditional fair field let to its demise from the great event it once was. A pleasure fair is still held, but on a site well out of the town.

The records for 1859 show that: *"Every description of horses except nags, were a dull sale; cart colts selling at fully 15% below last years prices. There were a few hacks on sale but at high prices. Two and three year a cart colts £25 to £35, suckers £13 to £16, draught horses £35 to £45."* The following year 20 Exmoor ponies sold for between £5 and £12 each and young team horses adapted for farming purposes fetched between £35 to £45.

A notable feature of the sheep sales that year was the disposal of the sale of the whole stock of the late Sir John Slade-Bart of Monty's Court Farm, near Taunton. The auctioneers were Messrs. Greenslades and Son of Taunton. The mottle faced flock, for which the Monty's Court Farm was famous, realized the following prices: breeding ewes 45st 46s, per head; hog ditto, 43s to 46s; wether hogs 46s to 46s; lambs 32s to 34s 6d.

Nearly 700 horses were exhibited at the 1881 fair cart colts averaging £45 while Exmoor ponies fetched between £6.00 and £8.00

Prices in 1893 were reported to have been lower than at the recent Westonzoyland fair with cart colts making £30 to £45 and hacks £18 to £25 with Exmoor ponies £3 to £5. It was noted that 4,747 sheep were penned, including a lot offered by Greenslade and Kidner of between 400 and 500, including 100 Dorset horn breeding ewes from Mr Edwin Kidner's Cothelstone flock.

In 1897 best Cart colts realised from £35 to £45 and hacks £45 while two magnificent colts which were awarded first prize at Bridgwater show were disposed of for £100 each. At least three auctioneers were selling stock that year, Messrs. Palmer & Snell. Mr. Horace Hurdman and Messrs. Greenslade & Kidner. The day started dull and by the afternoon rain fell heavily. There was almost a record number of sheep, nearly 7,000 and by late afternoon the field was a quagmire.

In 1902 cart colts made from £30 to £40, good hacks £30 and ponies £8 to £10. The following year prices were down slightly with cart colts making between £25 to £35.

The fair tolls from 1917 show that 6,807 sheep, 10 calves, 76 cattle and 254 horses were sold and the total toll revenue was just over £50.

By 1922 the figures were 4,292 sheep, 88 cattle and 308 horses. The business was described as being in a depression and a slump, with sheep numbers way down on previous years. During the 1920s a number of Irish hunters and hacks were offered for auction.

By 1930 the *Mercury* reports that the livestock business was by then confined to the one day and gave an insight into the years of the middle of the 19th century: *"The fair was almost the one occasion of the year when people from the countryside flocked in to Bridgwater for business purposes. Eighty years ago well to do people from the villages outside hastened in to Bridgwater, took a house for the fair week and made*

Above: Ponies driven from the Quantocks

many of their purchases for the coming year. In those days other amusements were provided by the old theatres and by the races held on Chilton common.

In those times too, some of the main streets such as High Street was a veritable market place during Fair week – were crowded with stalls, at which all kinds of commodities were sold."

In 1956 auctioneers R.B Taylor & Son disposed of many pens of Hampshire Down Lambs for which there was a keen demand. There was still a lively interest in the Horses in 1960 when yearling colts made from 31 to 34gns and Welsh colts and fillies 11 to 16 gns. 4,000 sheep were offered by R.B Taylor & Sons that year, which was the wettest fair for many years. The lamb trade was reported to be good with several pens making from £7 15s to £8 8s., best quality Ewes made from £9 to £10 5s.

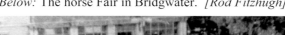

Below: The horse Fair in Bridgwater. *[Rod Fitzhugh]*

Pleasure Fair

Above: Three Helter Skelters feature at this Edwardian St. Matthews Fair. In the foreground are Heal's 4-breast Gallopers, a set of overboats with Hancock's and Anderton's Bioscope Shows. *[Rod Fitzhugh Collection]*

Up until the early 1870s the pleasure fair consisted of performances by strolling players, travelling theatre Mummers, Boxing Booths, Marionettes, Menageries or Wild Beast Shows, Wax Work, Peep Shows, Fortune Tellers, human and animal 'freaks', games of luck and skill and stalls selling food and vendors of comestibles offered from a tray such as Oysters, Pies, Gingerbread, intoxicating drinks and often patent medicines to cure all known ailments and even travelling dentists who charged a penny to watch them extract teeth. Wrestling was a popular sport at the fair with matches between local men and visiting opponents, as was boxing. Donkey racing was a boisterous and entertaining entertainment in the middle of the 19th century.

Gambling in many forms has been a popular, if illegal, pursuit at the fair for centuries. From the 19th century until the 1950s the ever vigilant Bridgwater constabulary has been seeking to combat illegal gaming and the press is peppered with accounts of tricksters being arrested at the fair for engaging in such outlawed games as the 'Three Card Trick' 'Crown and Anchor' and 'Prick the Garter'. Fraudsters were often arrested in West Street as well as in St Matthew's field.

The fate of the itinerant entertainer was guided by a series of 19th century acts of parliament that affected the way of life of travelling performers or showman and also banned some unsavoury pursuits hitherto enjoyed at fairs. The 1835 Cruelty to Animals Act outlawed cock-fighting and dog-fighting.

The 1834 Poor Law meant that travelling entertainers could be arrested for vagrancy. The following year the Highways act permitted street entertainments and sports to be reclassified as "nuisances". Travelling showfolk were put under pressure to confirm to the norm of late 19th century social order and settle in permanent dwellings. In 1889 the United Kingdom Van Dwellers Association was formed, the name of which was later changed to the Showman's Guild of Great Britain. The Guild was founded as a direct result of a campaign in parliament to restrict and licence all caravans, and successful opposition was organised by, and on behalf of, the showman who were the class chiefly affected. The proposed Moveable Dwellings Bill never became law and this objective achieved, the organisation was reconstituted on a national basis as a trade protection association. The Guild was set up to represent both fairground and circus showmen, indeed the first president was the famous circus impresario 'Lord' George Sanger. Both sectors of the travelling entertainment fraternity were represented by the Showmen's Guild before the war when the circus proprietors began to drift away and leave the Guild the preserve of the fairground showman. The last circus proprietor to be a Guild president was Bertram Mills.

The newspapers that served the town have always carried a report of St. Matthew's Fair, the emphasis being on the livestock sales until the end of the Second World War. These have, along with the showman's weekly newspaper the *World's Fair*, first published in 1904, provided a rich source of detailed accounts of the fair, the local press going back to the 1830's. The *Alfred* carried a report on the fair in 1832 and details the great lengths the town went to maintain law and order.

The *Alfred* October 1832: *"To prevent the dangerous consequences which might be fairly apprehended at this season from the crowds of strolling vagabonds which infest fairs, our magistrates have sworn in thirty special constables, who with the regular constabulary were employed in protecting the public from the inroads of these pests. Three persons were committed during the fair week for petty offences, and so successful were the precautionary measures taken that we have not heard of any of those instances of fraud and outrage which used* *to be so prevalent at St. Matthew's Fair. There were two rows of booths for the sale of intoxicating liquor. There was also a good deal of gambling and the police kept a watchful eye out for such games as thimble-rigging and pricking the garter."*

The lawlessness alluded to in 1832 is just a reflection of the sheer nastiness of life in Georgian England when fist and cudgel fighting was an everyday feature of life and an invitation to "put on the gloves" was as common as an exchange of pleasantries in the 20th century.

The fair in Victorian times was, on the whole, untroubled by violent or rowdy behaviour, the most common form of crime was pick pocketing, the perpetrators being described in the press as "the light fingered gentry". The borough police were diligent and strictly enforced the law regarding using obscene language or drunkenness in public. Gaming was unlawful and those involved were swiftly dealt with by the law.

Cloth from Yorkshire and the north was one of the most popular articles sold at the fair, farmers wives buying large amounts and putting it in store to supply the needs of their families until next Fair day. There was also on sale on stalls in St Matthew's Field clogs and ladies caps, straw bonnets, umbrellas, washing blue, corks, bungs, toys of every description, gingerbread,

Below: Shows, shooting galleries and the rides of Messrs. Heals and Hills at Bridgwater Fair before the Great War. *[Rod Fitzhugh]*

Above: Heal's 4-abreast Gallopers, Hill's Scenic Railway and Hancock's 4-abreast Gallopers to the left of the avenue and Richard's Razzle Dazzle to the right. *[Rod Fitzhugh]*

sweets, crockery in huge quantities, eatables of every description. There was also a large supply of ponies, horses, beasts, sheep, meat and every kind of agricultural produce

There were two circuses, one was the famous Ryan's Olympic Circus *[below]*. Lawrence's Theatre and Lismore's Theatre drew great crowds. The Lismores were of Irish descent and to illustrate how tight knit the travelling show community was, and indeed remains, one of the most notable West Country show families of the 20th century, the Whiteleggs, have the Lismores as descendents on the maternal side.

The 1847 fair failed to impress the reporter from the

Bridgwater Times: *"The fair commenced on Friday last, and was ushered in with about as miserable day as we can recollect for some time. The supply of fat cattle was good, but met with a dull sale at from 9s to 10s a score. Store cattle sold freely and at very high prices, but the supply was not good. In the sheep market the supply of fat sheep was great, meeting a ready sale at from 6d to 6 1/2d per lb. Cart colts fetched very high prices and were much sought after. As regards the fair itself, and its amusement we can say little. The shows were of the poorest kind, a few boxing booths, a learned pig, a few peep shows, mechanical exhibitions and a wandering thespian troupe completed the attractions; yet these appeared quite enough to satisfy the visitors."*

Many travelling entertainers simply carried their peep show by foot; a simple canvas front supported by a simple wooden framework, but most aspired to own a walk-up show, so called as the audience had to walk up a flight of wooden steps to reach the pay box, which was situated in the centre of an outside stage. This would be used by the flamboyant showman resplendent in top hat, spieling to the audience. He would be joined by a few musicians and a big bass drum and the clash of cymbals was an ever present feature. Clowns and dancing girls would attract the attention of the crowd, parading on the front of the show. The Peep show was more innocent an amusement than perhaps the name suggests. It was a

small booth with a canvas banner across the front presenting paintings of recent events such as battles or even gruesome murders and subsequent trials. The apparatus is splendidly described in the autobiography of the great Victorian showman Lord George Sanger: *"It had twenty six glasses so that twenty six people could see the views at the same time, the pictures being pulled up and down by strings. At night it was illuminated by a row of tallow candles set between the pictures and the observer, and requiring very regular snuffing. The pictures were about four feet by two feet and a half."*
The Peep show was popular until around 1854 when it was superseded by the Magic Lantern.

A splendid article in the *Bridgwater Times* portrays the fair of 1854 as the red letter day it was in the agricultural and social calendar of mid Victorian times. The *Times* was a new title first published in the town on 1st January 1846: *"On Monday morning our town presented a gay and animated appearance it being the commencement of the annual St. Matthew's Fair, The finesses of the weather was without precedent within our memories and induced a very large attendance of visitors. We are speaking within bounds when we state upwards of 10,000 persons visited Bridgwater on Monday. The Yeovil and Glastonbury Railways helped to swell the number. The field which, for years past, has been in a state of slush and mud was from the nature of the last*

crop, loose and friable. At a very early hour our streets were crowded with cattle and sheep on their way to the fair field...Dampiet Street and St Mary's Street, if not flowing with milk and honey, were bordered with many tons of cheese. The footway being covered to a depth of several feet and was the scene of much bustle and excitement. Towards ten o'clock the country people in their holiday attire poured into the town in an unbroken stream and droves of cattle were still being driven to the fair. At eleven the town seemed in danger of being besieged not by enemy but by visitors."

"During the afternoon the emigration was towards the fair and we may reasonably believe that Dame Durden had given her" men and maids" the day to enjoy themselves. If we could judge by the appearance of some of the buxom belles, tricked out with lace and ribbons in great profusion and by their ruddy cheeks and smiling faces, we would predict that care and privation were unknown to them."

"Every house appeared to be a 'public' and was decorated by signboards about 9 inches by 6 bearing the name of the "Inn" for the time being. The line of the march was studded with oyster stalls and just inside the entrance to the fair were a couple of cheap johns offering bargains to the gullible public. In the centre were shows, swings, roundabouts and all other etcs. which are considered as pertaining to the fair. A couple

Below: The corner of the ground by the *Horse and Jockey* with Marshall Hill's new Scenic Railway on the left and the side stalls of David Harrison and Harry Coneley, and Gratton's Boxing Booth. *[Rod Fitzhugh]*

Above: An impressive line up of riding machines including Symond's 4-abreast Gallopers, M. & B. Hill's Scenic and Anderton & Rowland's Steam Motors. *[Rod Fitzhugh]*

of travelling theatres amused the play going portion of the assembly with performances every half hour. The show people did not come out very extensively to gratify the pleasure seekers –the bad weather and consequent ill luck of previous years had discouraged the peripatetic exhibitors and collection of wild beasts, Moreland, horsemanship and even the penny peep shows were absent . We remember we used to follow the riders in their full dress procession through the town before their daily performances, and what dignity, to our young minds, it gave to St. Matthews Fair". We suppose the travelling monster circuses have swallowed up the mountebank exhibitions. At night the whole plain was lit up by 'portable gas'. Drinking booths were plentiful and the sound of ill used fiddle strings came from several."

"We had almost forgot the 'Goliath' at the fair, if we judge by his portrait outside, life size of course; he must have been at least 12 feet in height. Edibles of a substantial character were exposed in all directions to waylay the hungry or entrap the unwary. Frequently a beautiful blending of music would strike the ear, several bands playing at the same time, each pouring forth its own peculiar strain. We have been honoured by wandering minstrels, German bands and the time honoured Punch and his dog Toby, and a very creditable Puppet show. The light fingered gentry were

in full force. From 5,000 to 6,000 sheep were driven in and most sold for good prices."

In the *Bridgwater Times* account of the 1857 fair the amusements, according to the reporter, were not up to the normal standard, *"In this department there was generally a poor show. For students of natural history, there was an exhibition of reptiles &c. rendered attractive by its including 'the largest and handsomest woman in the world', and as a contrast 'the smallest women in the world', all to be seen for a very small sum."*

There were swinging boats and a huge stud of 'roundabout horses', the finest of the kind we have yet seen ' just imported from France' , bearing the names of the Crimean heroes; whilst there were booths in which to dance up the sides and down the middle."

The well known Moreland's Theatre had a competitor, Hambleton's in 1861, but the regular performer, Moreland, completely outshone his unpretending neighbour, his dresses more resplendent and he supplied for his outdoor public pantomimic characters whose antics greatly moved the risible faculties of the spectators."

The account also noted the particularly ambitious claims of one showman: *"In a small caravan carrying a vast surface of pictorial canvas, there were announced for view the largest and smallest women in the world,*

13

Lilliputian animals of all kinds, a real sea-serpent and other things, too numerous to mention. How the little vehicle could hold this precious assembly of notables and yet find accommodation for some 50 people willing to transfer the ownership of one penny, many bystanders were puzzled to understand and invested a copper to solve the problem."

After the livestock, cheese was the main commodity traded at the 1858 fair with best red selling for 60s per cwt and best white 67 to 70s per cwt.

The Pleasure fair was dismissed as *"penny peep shows, sparring booths and tawdry theatricals."* Drinking booths, it was noted, outnumbered the shows. The *Independent* added rather haughtily *"If the thousands who flocked to the fair were satisfied with the treats prepared for them we can only say that they are exceedingly moderate in their expectations."*

The 1859 fair was once again spoiled by *"the wretched weather"* but the visitors to the town were as determined as ever to enjoy the delights the fair had to offer. The *Times* commented somewhat disparagingly on the amusements on offer. *"The votaries of various kinds of amusement had their desires excited if not gratified. We might turn from the disgusting semi nudity of the pugilist or from the awful three act tragedy to the young equestrians on the rotatory horses that, so docile as not to require rarefying or imagine yourself in the*

presence of Venus's by gazing on the rouged beauties of the stage. Among the more ridiculous entertainments at the fair several men with machines for testing the strength of the lungs, for the use of which they charged a halfpenny. These are samples of the kind of amusement offered to the public of the present day at most of our fairs, but is hoped that the great St. Matthew's Fair will, in course of time become, as in earlier times, a great market only." Messrs. Maynard's offered for auction 60 greatly admired Exmoor ponies, the property of Henry Matthews, prices ranging from £8 to £34.

In 1860 Equestrian displays, performing pigs and monkeys and the exhibition of a giant were on offer in the fair the main draw being Moreland's theatre. The exploits at Garibaldi and the recent scenes at the Agapemone were among the representations exhibited. Moreland was nothing if not topical; poking fun at the Agapemone religious community at nearby Spaxton was a very popular pastime among the working classes at the time. While the exploits of the sect founded by Henry Prince and Samuel Starkey, two former Church of England clergyman in 1850, scandalised the middle and upper classes they became targets of ridicule amongst most country folk. Prince claimed that the Holy Ghost had taken up residence in his body and his followers proclaimed that the second coming was imminent. There were more women than men in the sect and it was

Below: A line up of shows at Bridgwater, including Sing Fu, Tiny Tim and Lola the strange girl! *[DeVey family]*

14

notorious during the 1850s and 60's. Each house was permitted to sell liquor without licence during the three days of the fair.

"The old privilege of selling beer without licence during the fair was adopted by numerous of the inhabitants of West Street and by the aid of a barrel of beer, a cracked fiddle many drove a flourishing trade, back kitchens and upstairs rooms being thronged with rustics, who imbibed beer and danced jigs with young ladies who rejoiced in the most capacious of crinolines and most flaming of head dresses , but whose morals, like many other things in this world , will not bear investigation." However the following year the licensing laws were reformed and the "bush houses" as they were known were prohibited from selling beer. A marked improvement was visible in West Street in consequence of the abolition of the bush houses. In former years nearly every house was a beer shop, but now the new Licensing Act prohibits it and the law was duly observed.

Freak shows or 'Exhibitions of Human Oddities' were a popular attraction in less politically correct times and often a person with a deformity or of extreme height or girth could earn a healthy living from exhibiting themselves. The exhibition of bizarre curiosities–both living and dead, animal and human was a thriving industry in the 18th and 19th centuries. Society fetes such as the Hyde Park Fete in London to country mops and fairs such as Bridgwater had a regular supply of 'Fat Ladies', 'Living Skeletons', 'Giant and Dwarfs', 'Spotted Boys' as well as six legged sheep or two headed calves. Often these unfortunate freak animals were sold at birth to showman and survived for only a short time. After death they were often preserved in jars and exhibited.

The most famous 'freak' to be exhibited in Victorian England was Joseph Merrick, known as 'the Elephant Man'. Merrick was born in Leicestershire in 1862, with severe deformities to the head, to poor parents and was soon abandoned to an orphanage. After being passed from one showman to another, Merrick, suffering from general ill health was taken in by Tom Norman and exhibited in a shop in London's East End. The shop was opposite the London Hospital and a surgeon named Frederick Treves came to his aid. Treves examined Merrick and later wrote, *"The poor fellow was deformed in body face, head and limbs. His skin thick and pendulous, hung in folds and resembled the hide of an elephant-hence his show name.".* Under the care of Treves, John Merrick's health returned and his confidence grew and he was sheltered from ridicule.

There is no doubt from contemporary accounts that Merrick's show life was a miserable one, but given the prejudices that existed then, Norman offered the only food and shelter available to him. John Merrick's deformities were at the extreme scale and certainly those

noted that the women were either rich or beautiful. The sect was shrouded in secrecy and the Agapemone, which translated as *"abode of love"* was behind high walls. Gossip of a scandalous nature spread like wild fire. There were many instances of Prince arranging marriages of rich young women with sect members and of some of the women leaving when pregnant and at least one who was incarcerated in the local lunatic asylum.

Members of the sect were noted as handing out their literature at the fair during the time it was in existence. In fact the public was offered literature from many different societies ranging from the various Temperance groups, Gospel Missions, Bible Society and many other Evangelical groups. According to contemporary accounts there was little interest in the literature offered by such groups.

A tame and trained Seal was billed as *"The Talking Fish"* at the 1861 fair. The *Mercury* reported: *"Many hundreds visited his tent during Thursday. It was captured by some fisherman at Port Isaac in the Bristol Channel, in January last. It is remarkably tame, and at the bidding of his master will perform numerous feats such as kiss him, comb his hair and answer questions in a peculiar voice."* A rival for the penny admission was a wonderfully intelligent pony, whose feats eclipsed that of Toby, the learned Pig. The report goes on to allude to the activities in West Street, which had become

Above: Heal's 4-abreast, Marshall Hill's Switchback, Hancock's Show and Anderton & Rowland's Cinematograph with the engines, living wagons and packing trucks in the foreground. *[Rod Fitzhugh]*

with lesser disabilities and midgets, giants and fat women were able to negotiate, even dictate terms and conditions that made their earnings far in excess of other working people at that time.

The gullible public were often hoodwinked with claims of the showman to see the 'smallest pony' or the 'largest rat in the world'. The smallest pony was usually a Shetland sheared of its shaggy coat making it look smaller and shown standing in a pit in deep straw where people looked down on it. The 'largest rat' was usually a coypu.

In 1832 an enterprising showman exhibited a shaved monkey as a fairy and during the same decade a shaven faced bear was exhibited as a 'pig faced women'. Fat girls, bearded or tattooed ladies, midgets and dwarves billed as "Leprechauns" were still popular up until the late 1950s. Instances of those with physical deformities exhibiting themselves surprisingly persisted after the establishment of the Welfare State in 1946. As late as 1950 Tommy Jacobsen appeared in a side shows in the West Country, billed as *"the armless wonder"* where he played piano threw darts and performed other tasks using his toes. Tommy Jacobsen was the last such "freak" entertainer, before a more enlightened age emerged..

Local historian Roger Evans has discovered a much earlier example of a local person born with no arms who was exhibited at the fairs of Somerset and almost certainly St. Matthew's. Sarah Biffen born to farm labourers in the village of East Quantoxhead in 1784 was bound for sixteen years and exhibited by travelling showmen named Dukes. Sarah had taught herself to sew her own clothes and learnt how to paint using her mouth. Sarah who grew to be only 37 inches tall, had an extraordinary gift as an artist and painted with oils. While at the famous St. Bartholomew's Fair at Smithfield in London in 1808 her talent caught the eye of the Earl of Morton who took on the role of patron , and arranged for tuition under William Craig, the Queen's painter under the Earl's patronage. Sarah worked from a studio in London's prestigious Bond Street where she was patronised by royalty became a society figure and was even mentioned in Charles Dickens Nicholas Nickleby.

There is a handbill in the British Museum which reads: *"This Young Lady was born deficient of arms hands and Legs; she is of comely appearance and 25 years old and only 37 inches high. She displays a great genius, and is an admirer of the arts, but what renders her so worthy of public notice is the industrious and astonishing means she has invented and practised in obtaining the use of needle scissors, pen and pencil. She can cut out and make her own clothes, writes well and, draws landscapes, paints miniatures and many other wonderful things, all of which principally she does with her mouth. The reader may think it impossible that she should be capable of doing what is inserted in this bill., but if she cannot, the conductor will forfeit 1,000 guineas. Open from Twelve O' Clock in the forenoon. Pit 1s, Gallery 6d .NB Miniature likenesses painted on ivory at Three Guineas each"* Dukes appeared to have exploited Sarah as she was allowed just £5 per year.

At first glance the exhibiting of human "freaks" appears to exemplify the worst excesses and ignorances of our Victorian ancestors. The showman is seen as a callous opportunist exploiting the unfortunate and appealing to the prurient voyeuristic tendencies of the public. Contemporary accounts however, show that showmen and their human exhibits generally struck mutually advantageous deals.

Paying to stare at "human oddities" as they were known was not confined to the working classes, indeed Queen Victoria had a keen interest in the subject and there are many examples of such 'oddities', including P.T Barnum's famous dwarf, 'Major' Tom Thumb and others who exhibited themselves being presented to the Queen and her court. In 1847 a dwarf, advertised as

GENERAL TOM THUMB,
THE "GREAT LITTLE MAN."

Below: Johnny Gratton's throwing game. Five large faces were painted on banners and players had to try to knock the teeth out with balls. The swag is displayed on the shelves below. With Gratton are his wife, Selina, and daughter Ruby. *[Rosie Small]*

Above: Heal's 4-abreast Gallopers amongst the line of machines at Bridgwater. *[Rod Fitzhugh]*

being 'the real American Tom Thumb' was exhibited during St. Matthew's Fair week in the public rooms in George Lane, not on the fairground. The General Tom Thumb was exhibited by that most famous of American showmen P.T Barnum and the General and Barnum were the best of friends and split their profits 50/50. The admission price to see Tom Thumb in 1847 was a shilling for adults and 6d for children. A lot of money when the rest of the show booths charged a penny. They toured the country by train, travelling first class and appearing at towns with a famous fair or as a sole novelty attraction if none were taking place staying at the grand homes of Barnum's network of society friends or at the finest hotel in the town.

The magic lantern show was another popular feature on the Victorian fairground and in the home. This had been around in some form since the 17th century and enjoyed a concurrent vogue from the 1860s. In the hands of the flamboyant showmen a great spectacle could be produced, with either sickly sweet Victorian sentimentality or bone chilling tales of terror of the most macabre nature. The Ghost Show was a spectacular illusion using real actors appearing as spectral apparitions floating across the stage, an elaborate optical illusion created by a sheet of glass placed at an angle of 45 degrees on which a light was shone; the actors were concealed on a platform below the stage.

The Ghost show was one of the most extravagant and successful illusions shows to appear on the fair and was based on the illusion of 'Peppers Ghost' which was first shown in London in 1862 and was quickly adapted by travelling showmen as well as the permanent theatre. The Ghost show reached the peak of popularity in the 1870s. It caused a real sensation when first shown at the fair. Contemporary reports tell of ladies fainting and the audience screaming with a mixture of laughter and fear as the showman conjured up the apparitions seemingly from thin air as he spun the audience a bone chilling tale often weaving local legend or superstition into the tale he told. So enduring is this classic British invented illusion that some of the biggest names in the American theme park industry still use it in their dark rides and shows. But the people of Bridgwater first saw the illusion in splendidly appointed Victorian show booths in the 1860s.

The Bridgwater *Independent* in October 1863 reports that the growth of the Pleasure fair in recent years was due to the change of dates of Barnstaple Great Fair to avoid a clash. This arrangement was clearly to the great advantage of the show folk. Barnstaple charter fair is held approximately two weeks before Bridgewater and many of the same showmen in the latter part of the 19th century attended both fairs. Using horses, the railway or showman's road locomotives they would leave Barnstaple on Saturday the day after the fair finished and travel to Taunton to 'fill in' for a week and spend time repainting and varnishing their equipment in readiness for Bridgwater. Great use was made of the railway by stall holders and smaller traders and showmen.

In the 1920's there were regularly two fairs in Taunton competing for business in the week prior to St. Matthew's. The firm of Anderton & Rowland opened on the more favourable Jarvis's Field (now the cattle mart) at the Station road end of the town, while Hill Brothers would open on the Poor Ground (now the site of the Bus depot) in Hamilton road to the east of the less prosperous part of the town in those days.

The lessee of St. Matthew's Fair Field during the 1860s was Mrs Kirk, the Landlady of the Tynte Inn, Pigs Cross. The coverage of the 1863 fair in the *Independent* recorded a dispute between Mrs. Kirk and a showman: *"Under Mrs Kirks superintendence or that of her agent, the disposal of the booths & takes place. It is customary for the proprietors of these, too, in order to secure a favourable standing ground, to send a deposit to the lessee, and point out at the same time on which site they wish to stand. Now Isaac Gregory is the proprietor of a couple of exhibitions and some months ago he sent the lessees a deposit of 10 shillings, and the lessee in return , guaranteed him a certain spot of ground on which to erect his tent. Subsequently, however she for the same received a deposit from two other show proprietors for the same ground. The consequence of which on the first day a serious altercation took place between the parties."* The matter was only settled in the court and Isaacs was fined £7 for obstruction.

One of the main attractions on the fair field that year was Baker's Circus, which distributed handbills announcing that a performer would walk a tight rope from the ground to the top of the tent. The Fairs and Markets Superintendent, Lear, deemed this to be dangerous and illegal and applied to the Mayor who directed him to proceed at once to the Fair Field and prevent the performance from taking place. Baker, on being told the performance was illegal, admitted to the superior force of the law and submitted. Thankfully this over zealous stewardship of the fair was short lived and in the following years circus artistes were left to perform at their own risk.

Baker's Circus was a popular and successful Bristol based company of acrobats, bareback riders, tightrope walkers and clowns. As well as appearing at fairgrounds the circus would open at the towns of the West Country to coincide with the opening of the

Below: Anderton & Rowland's Gondolas and Marshall Hill's Switchback and Helter Skelter at Bridgwater in 1912. *[Rosie Small]*

assizes.

1863 was the first year a steam powered ride appeared on a fairground in Yorkshire, but St. Matthew's Fair in that year consisted of swings and roundabouts propelled by ponies and small boys, travelling theatres, including Baker's and Moreland's, and several boxing booths. Moreland's theatre was a portable wooden building with a large canvas-painted front, run by George Moreland, who played the leading parts, Harry Moreland played the villain and Ben Moreland the low comedian. Moreland's theatre visited Taunton during the assizes. Their repertoire included Hamlet, Othello, and other Shakespeare plays.

The other attractions included gingerbread stalls, Punch and Judy booths, oyster vendors, toy and cutlery dealers as well as several booths licensed for the sale of intoxicating liquor. The main business of the fair in the 1860s was the sale of cattle, horses, ponies, sheep and cheese was a commodity of major commercial importance.

The clemency of the weather was the main factor in the success of the 1867 fair, the previous year's being marred by inclement weather, the fair *"well stocked with shows etc"* The fair was *"ankle deep in mud"* in 1868 with rain falling heavily on the Wednesday although this did not deter the farmer's dealers or those on pleasure bent, with a large number of shooting galleries and shows. Those engaged in gambling where ordered off the field by the police and two card sharps were taken into custody.

Oysters, although considered a gourmet treat today, were a very plentiful cheap and popular source of protein in the 19th century. There was a very brisk trade in the sought after Bridgwater cloth at this time, always thought of as being superior to Taunton cloth.

In 1870 the Female Blondin and her far-famed troupe of male and female artistes performed 'death defying feats' in a circus tent at the fair, including tight rope walking. The female Blondin was circus artiste 'Madame' Mary Biddall, a member of a well known show family. She performed with the world famous French wire walker Blondin.

In 1871 foot and mouth disease had broken out in the county leading to a reduced number of cattle for auction. The change in the way cattle were bought and sold was reported upon in the *Mercury* in October 1872 and in a rather gloomy leading article warned of the danger of the fair falling in to a spiral of decline: *"The growth in weekly cattle marts which has led to a gradual decline of town and country fairs. Although the sheep market continued to prosper there had been a marked reduction in the number of cattle entered. This is not to be wondered at, seeing the establishment of weekly cattle markets and the increased facilities offered for the removal of stock from and to any part of the kingdom, by fulfilling the purpose the fairs were intended to serve we*

have effectively got rid of the necessity for holding them. The non-observance of ancient customs, however useless they may have become, is a source of regret to some persons, and the entire abolition of St. Matthews fair in Bridgwater, whilst it would not, for the reasons above stated, seriously interfere with the disposal of grazed stock in this neighbourhood, would doubtless occasion great disappointment to a large number of adults as well as juveniles who have been accustomed to regard it as their annual holiday."

"A very satisfactory feature in connection with last weeks fair was an undoubted decrease in drunkenness and of the scenes of riot and dissipation which disgraced former occasions of a similar nature. Prior to 1867 when the date was altered from 2nd October to the last Wednesday in September and when a "fair Sunday" sometimes intervened , the occupants of almost every house in West Street were permitted to sell liquor , and dancing and every kind of revelry were carried on to the disgust and annoyance of every respectable person. This custom has almost died out the result being that West Street, which was formerly filled with drunken and other loose people, is now nearly as quiet during the fair as any other thoroughfare in the town .The closing of the drinking booths in the fair at eleven O'clock has also had a very wholesome effect . All this is a matter of congratulation and encourages the hope that St. Matthew's Fair, however much it may be shorn of its original commercial importance, will in future years gain a good repute and be less productive of evil than heretofore."

The industrial revolution brou ght steam power to the fair and a new dimension to the spectacle of the fair, electric light. The arrival of the steam driven roundabouts revived the fortunes of the fair over the next two decades. The fierce competition between showmen for rights at fairs strengthened St. Matthew's position. The day at the fair, already a well earned and looked forward to holiday, now of offered scenes of utter enchantment as dusk fell. Thousands of twinkling fairy lights in a kaleidoscope of colours reflected in cut glass mirrors and shining brass fitments on merry-go-rounds and traction engines. The prominent showmen of South Wales and the Midlands established rights at rival fairs such as Gloucester Barton leaving those based in Bristol and Plymouth to establish rights at Bridgwater, Barnstaple and Glastonbury. The introduction of electric light on the fairground coupled with the new steam driven roundabouts proved to be a huge draw for country folk.

Galloping Horse Steam Circuses, as the first roundabouts were first known, emulated the movements of a galloping horse by means of an overhead crank. The Victorians liked to look back in history for inspiration in not only trends in architecture and home decoration but also in their entertainment. Hence the

Above: Hancock's 4-abreast Galloping Horses. *[Martin Burridge]*

wooden mounts on the Galloping Horse roundabout became Knights chargers. The Victorians had a great deal of romanticism for the medieval period. It was their form of nostalgia. The advent of the great steam roundabout and its successor the opulent and fantastically gilded Switchbacks coincided with the highest period in history of hand craftsmanship, the late Victorian period. The level of craftsmanship that went into these huge gilded structures was breathtaking. Venetian Gondolas with hand carved cars and marvellously embellished panels with bevelled mirrored rounding boards. That was just on the aesthetic side. The engineering was just as impressive. Driven by a centre steam engine and built up and hauled to the fair by mighty steam driven traction engines with canopies supported by gleaming twisted brass rods. Often these loads, as many as eight or nine, were transported by rail and collected from the station by the traction engines. From the late 19th century as part of the industrial revolution the pleasure fair was transformed from being just a venue for circus performers, travelling theatre and freak shows by the invention of the great steam roundabout. These lavish creations must have left the visitors from outlying villages in a sense of awe. The firm of W.C. & S. Hancock were pioneers of the steam roundabout in the west and the firm became a household name from Bristol to Penzance. Their array of show tackle was so great that they had depots at Bristol and later Plymouth. They purchased their first steam roundabout from Frederick Savage of King's Lynn. It is recorded in the factory engine register as no. 185 new double cylinder engine for four-abreast steam circus for W. &C. Hancock and dated 1877. Hancock's took delivery of the Roundabout in November 1878. Savage was both an agricultural and roundabout engineer of great ingenuity and the most famous of the English roundabout makers.

This was the beginning of the fair as we know it with the arrival of the first rides. A chance to sit in plush upholstered Venetian gondolas or whirl round on a galloping wooden horse to the exciting brass, woodwind and percussion notes of a military band organ, a pleasing contrast no doubt to the creaking harmonium at weekly chapel. During the late 19th century working people from rural areas led a harsh frugal existence mostly living in cramped draughty cottages with no sanitation and lit only by candles.

A drunken circus musician was brought before the bench in 1879. James Coggin, a clarinet player at Baker's circus in the fair field, was charged with drunkenness on the previous night in West Street. P.C. Gooderidge said, *"It was a very bad case, not only had he (witness) turn to him out from court after court where he annoyed the inhabitants but he struck one man in the face and was guilty of indecent exposure."* The fair that year was very muddy, shows were very few and of an inferior description.

Famous West Country show woman Sophia Hancock the sister of William and Charles charged Phillippa Birchall, 32, with threatening her with violence during the 1882 fair. Miss Hancock, 27, described as *"the keeper of a shooting–gallery and single woman living in Bristol"*, complained to the police that Phillippa Birchall had *"threatened her"*. The court heard that the pair met at 11, 0 clock at night in the fair field. The defendant called Miss. Hancock everything she could and threatened to *"pull her wind pipe out"*. She also asked her to *"have a round with her"*. Witness was afraid she would do her some bodily injury. In cross examination, complainant said she had been afraid of the defendant several years. They had had words before. P.C. Selway gave corroborative evidence, adding that he had heard defendant say to complainant that one of them would lose their life before the night was over. Mr Chapman, representing Phillippa Birchall, urged that it was a case of *"six of one and half a dozen of the other"*. Defendant was bound over in her own recognisance of £5 and her husband's surety in a like sum to keep the peace for six months. In an earlier case the same day Tom and Phillippa pleaded guilty to creating a public annoyance in the fair field the previous night and were fined 2s 6s plus costs.

Thomas and Phillippa Birchall were a pair of very colourful characters and were brought before the bench more than once for domestic quarrels. Thomas was from Lancashire and his wife a Cornish woman. They wintered in St. Austell and in the early 1880s travelled a shooting gallery around the fairs of the West Country and later a Peep show or Fine Art Gallery. The Birchalls became well known members of the West Country show fraternity.

By 1886 the first steam driven Galloping Horse roundabouts had started to appear. The *Independent's* account of that year's event is more general than usual. Roundabouts had been common since the mid-19th century but the mechanism to emulate a horse galloping

Below: Thomas Birchall and his family travelled a Shooting Gallery along with a steam-driven Dobby Set. The shooter is shown in this view, along with their Brown & May showman's engine. *[Jeanette Broadway]*

22

Above: The parading girls out on the stage on Hancock's Cinematograph Show. *[Rosie Small]*

was patented in 1885. There were, as customary, a large number of roundabouts, swings and shooting galleries, and several shows. A number of games of chance, one of them of rather a questionable character, were practised at intervals and the police had to interfere in a few instances, although the fair passed off quietly and without any great disturbances.

One of the owners of St. Matthew's Field, Mr. Bouverie was contacted by the Markets Committee in September 1886 to see if a wall could be erected *"on that portion of the field which abuts against the highway between the* Horse and Jockey *and the western end of the field, in lieu of the present hedge and bank"*.

The nature of some of the shows was brought in to question by the *Independent* in 1888: *"Some of the exhibitions in the field, as usual, were of a most indelicate nature, and we think the authorities should use their power to suppress those features of the fair which undeniably tend to demoralise the young people that witness them."*

Prominent local brewers Starkey Knight and Ford had a strong presence at the fair at this time, with three beer tents in addition to two other tents run by Jeffrey Denman and Mrs. Lovibond. Starkey Knight & Ford was founded in 1852 and had its head office in Tiverton. It had a substantial brewery in the town and became one of the largest regional brewers in the country, supplying its large pub estate across the west. It was acquired by

Whitbread in 1962 and the Bridgwater brewery in Northgate closed in 1964. Its familiar galloping black horse trademark was a common sight on pubs and hotels.

Purchases Queen's Waxworks Exhibition was the largest show in 1889. The *Independent* reported that *"Alongside this was Newman's Circus and among the 'living wonders' exhibited were a remarkably fat woman, a wonderful double bodied girl, an English Giant Horse and an Arabian steed with five legs, the educated pony, American performing birds and a performing monkey as was the Alpine Railway, the later novelty attracting much attention. Wildman's and Hancock's Galloping Horses were extensively patronised. Drinking booths, shooting galleries, photographic studios, donkeys from Burnham and Weston Super Mare and Punch and Judy also found plenty of patrons. The boxing booth this year was conspicuous by absence, and in its place in a remote corner of the field was utilized as an encampment for the Salvation Army."* Donkey rides provided some end of season business for those operating such businesses at Burnham and Weston Super Mare for many years.

The *Independent* reported there were four big shows in 1890 including: *"A military exhibition and a performing dogs and monkeys entertainment. There was the usual collection of roundabouts, shooting galleries, etc. and the Alpine Railway. William Plumb, a young man in the employment of Hancock's the roundabout proprietors, who in endeavouring to save a child who was falling off a horse, was caught by a hook and his elbow was torn away very severely."*

In 1892 Hancock's, who had introduced the steam driven galloping horse roundabout to the fair in 1879, presented to the public an even more elaborate machine the steam Switchback.

The ride had the most elaborately carved rounding boards and a new Burrell showman's engine *Pride of the West* was purchased to haul the loads. The roundabout was powered by a steam engine mounted in the centre of the ride. Passengers sat in gilded chariot-like cars, of which there were eight. The *Mercury* reported that *"Hancock's Steam Switchback railway proved a great novelty and attraction and was even more extensively patronised than the ordinary roundabouts."*

The following year one of the most famous showmen of the era appeared at the fair for the first time, Professor Anderton, with his conjuring establishment -Anderton's Home of Mysteries. This was the stage name of Albert Haslam born in Chesterfield in 1851. Haslam took his name from one of great Victorian illusionists and conjurors, Professor Anderson, the Great Wizard of the North, with whom he had worked and was his mentor. Anderson was admired by and was a friend of that greatest of all showmen, the American P.T Barnum, a frequent visitor to Britain at this time.

Anderton's show was new the previous year and opened out to present a 44ft. frontage, richly gilded with gold leaf. Professor Anderton was also a noted hypnotist and was described by contemporary accounts as *"A prince of showman"* and a '*genius*'. The show caused a sensation wherever it opened and in 1894 performing lions were introduced to the show presided over by Anderton's 23 year-old son Arthur, who assumed the name 'Captain Rowland.' Their advert for the rather grandly titled 'Anderton & Haslam's Royal No.1 Menagerie &Combined Shows' claimed that Captain Rowland would *"fight the untameable lions."*

After appearing at Bridgwater in 1895 the show was touring the villages of Somerset and at Martock in the south of the county in mid November when one of the lions escaped. The incident was reported in the *Mercury* of 20 November 1895: *"Considerable excitement was caused in Martock on Wednesday when one of the lions belonging to Anderton &Haslam's Menagerie had got out of its cage. Whilst the attendants were at tea they heard the elephant screaming and found one of lions at large and running up and down inside the menagerie. Captain Rowland the lion tamer was at once summoned and both he and Mr Anderton Jnr. saw that it would be*

Below: Anderton & Haslam's band wagon hauled by their elephant and camels. *[DeVey family]*

Bridgwater Mercury, 1894

unwise to capture the animal and decided to shoot it. Captain Rowland then got on top of one of the caravans and shot it from there. *The animal, one of a four, was purchased about six months since from Carl Hagenbeck at the Crystal Palace for about £500. Great praise is due to Captain Rowland and the proprietor for the prompt manner in which they acted in the interest of public safety."* Captain Rowland thought the accident occurred through carelessness of one of the attendants.

Animated pictures were added to the show in 1897 and the name of the show changed to Anderton & Rowland's. Mander's Waxwork Exhibition was the *"most conspicuous"* attraction in 1892 and the boxing booth offered the chance to fight some well known prize fighters. Other exhibitions included a 'Wild Women' and an 'Oriental Beauty'. Hancock's roundabout and Switchback railway were kept in constant motion. Ladies *teasers* were in great request, affording amusement to the many and, annoyance to the few, who however bore it good humouredly.

A 'Strong Woman' who lifted a horse was the talk of

the 1893 fair along with a sparring booth in which visitors were invited to wrestle with a bear, there were two Marionette shows and Hancock's Switchback and two roundabouts. An interesting feature of the enforcement of law and order is revealed in the *Mercury's* report of that year. It would appear that retired Police officers were drafted in to support the regular officers on duty. Some card sharps and light fingered gentry were spotted by ex-Inspector Cheriton and other superannuated members of the borough police whose services had been very wisely requisitioned by Supt. Barnett. The account of the event also mentions another regular feature in late Victorian times, Members of the Gospel Mission occupied a platform at the entrance of the field, delivering addresses and singing hymns. These along with members of the temperance movement were ever present to warn fair goers against the perils of excessive enjoyment or the dangers of strong drink. The show folk had their own religious services often using the grand organs on the shows and roundabouts to accompany the hymn singing.

The atrocious weather that preceded the 1894 fair was responsible for the Hancock's giving Bridgwater a miss that year and travelling to Gloucester to open at that city's famous Barton Fair, the date of which clashed with Bridgwater. The Mercury reported that *"rain fell heavily during the three preceding days and the owners of the allotment grounds had just dug up their crop of potatoes there was every expectation that the portion allotted to the shows would be a quagmire. The prospect of this was so disheartening to the proprietor of Hancock's famous roundabouts and switchback railway that failing to obtain the use of the ground adjoining, where wheat had been grown and in far better condition, he determined to proceed to Gloucester fair instead and to the disappointment of many his example was followed by the proprietors of many shows as well, fortunately the weather on Wednesday and Thursday turned out much better than anticipated and the ground not as muddy as was feared. The attractions of the fair were very few, the only redeeming feature being a menagerie, which was largely attended."*

Fortune smiled on Professor Anderton and Captain Rowland as they had invested in a large advertisement in the Mercury and most of the competition had gone to Gloucester fair.

The advert promised *"the most complete, Novel and Instructive Exhibition ever seen in this Country"* and featured a performing elephant among a whole host of performers.

Excitement at the anticipation of the appearance of *"an enormous revolving wheel, an imitation of the one at Earls Court"* in 1895 turned to disappointment when the wheel advertised by placards two weeks previously failed to present itself. The *Mercury* noted *"The loss was compensated for to a certain extent by Messrs.*

Hancock's sets of roundabouts and Spanish Gondolas, which were brought to the field by two traction engines, and were decidedly the centre of attraction. The largest of these roundabouts with four horses a breast, was fitted up in most gorgeous and costly manner and the employment of the revolving electric light was great acquisition. The gondolas were very handsome cars, and a capital substitute for the switchback."

The exhibition that year included Proctor's circus, a 'Spanish menagerie' in which *"a capital specimen of a sea lion was on view and a man of colour entered a lion's den, which we fear (in view of the apparent ferocity of the animal) he will do once too often,"* Barnum's Living Novelties", Taylor's Venice in London with a representation of the China and Japan War.

An attraction at one of the boxing booths was the special engagement of Joe and Tom Wilson of Leicester, the light weight champions of England. and to another the contest between some female boxers. The roundabouts soon pushed the shows to the perimeter of the fairground and became the prime attractions. The fairground had begun its transformation from a place where shows were presented to a venue for riding roundabouts and switchbacks. These huge machines and their attendant steam traction engines were transported to Bridgwater by rail and then to the fairground by the engines.

Many visitors to the fair arrived by railway. The Bristol to Exeter railway opened a station to the east of the town in 1841, the same year that Bridgwater docks were opened. A second station, known as Bridgwater North, was opened by the Somerset & Dorset railway in 1890 and ran a branch line from Eddington, this closed in 1952. Hundreds of people from Glastonbury and Street and the villages along the line on the Somerset levels poured into the town on fair day.

The report from the 1897 fair in the Bridgwater *Mercury* gives a flavour of the fairground during the latter part of the 19th century: *"The Pleasure fair was very plentifully supplied with shows, roundabouts, swings, shooting galleries etc. Although the fair is no longer attended by theatrical companies like those of Morelands and Weights, which several years ago were its chief attraction, the shows on this occasion were more numerous than usual. They included a Circus where the Talking Horse was the principle feature; a Menagerie on a small scale in which some very daring feats were performed by Marco a coloured man [Crecraft's Show] who struggled with a lion and threw it on its back, and afterwards had a boxing match with a large bear; an exhibition of a fat women and a midget; a sparring booth in which the noble art was practised; and another menagerie Biddall Brothers, on a much larger scale where a dwarf had a glove encounter with a kangaroo, and two lion tamers risked their lives with the caged beasts. One of these tamers, earlier in the day,* was savagely attacked and bitten by a lioness, which had to be beaten off. The injured man was compelled to have the wounds dressed by a surgeon, but not withstanding this, he boldly ventured into the cage again in the evening.

Hancock's magnificent sets of Roundabouts and Gondolas (brilliantly illuminated with electric light), were as usual very extensively patronised. The shooting galleries and Indian Jungles were fairly well supported. The pastime of shying at coconuts was largely indulged in; others tested their strength by means of a sledge hammer, fortunes were told by caged birds; and fruit and confectionery stalls were well patronised as were the various refreshment booths provided by licensed victuallers in the town, and in respect of which special licenses had been obtained. On the whole giving the severe inclemency of the weather, St Matthew's Fair was this year in all respects a very successful one."

A further sensation was caused in 1897 by a local Publican, Mr E.K Lloyd of the Punch Bowl accepting a challenge from Mr Biddall, proprietor of the Menagerie to "Enter the lions den". The Mercury reported: *"The announcement attracted a large number of persons who would not have otherwise visited it, and the Menagerie was very much more patronised. In consequence, another special attraction being the employment on this occasion of the Bridgwater Borough Band under the conductorship of Mr F. Purches. The knowledge that Mr Lloyd had entered the establishment shortly before nine o clock caused considerable excitement and considerably increased the number of admissions. The proprietor announced that Mr Lloyd had voluntarily offered, and at his own risk to enter the den with him and asked that silence be observed. The tamer first entered the cage containing a lion and lioness, Mr Lloyd immediately followed and as soon as they were shut in a hearty cheer was raised, but silence was again commanded and maintained for the space of three or four minutes, during which time Mr Lloyd coolly lighted a cigar, and stroked the head of the lion, also shaking hands with his companion. On Mr Lloyd emerging from the cage, he was cheered most enthusiastically and the proprietor intimated that he should have much pleasure in forwarding a medal commemorative of the event, which he remarked was another example of 'true British pluck'. Mr Lloyd received another ovation by the crowd assembled on the outside on leaving the menagerie."*

A major development that was to dominate the entertainment scene in the 20th century was first witnessed on the fairgrounds in 1897: the moving picture or Silent Movie. A development from the magic lantern and" What the Butler Saw" Mutoscopes. The moving picture was first demonstrated by the Lumiere brothers on 22nd March 1895 on their Cinematographe. One of the first to develop Moving pictures on the fairgrounds was West Country Showman William

Above: Anderton's Grand Empire Palace was the rather grandiose name given to their travelling show. The dancing girls are on the front stage, the fair organ on the left provides the music, and the steam engine generates the power.

Taylor, born in Wiltshire in 1853. The leading show family of the day W. C. & S. Hancock introduced animated pictures in 1897. Anderton & Rowland also added moving pictures that year. The Electrograph Bioscope was then incorporated into Hancock's Menagerie and Variety Show. In 1900 the Menagerie was rebuilt as the Palace of Varieties and Living Pictures and an 87 key Gavioli Organ replaced the older barrel organ. A Burrell Showman's Road Locomotive, *Her Majesty*, formed part of the elaborate show front; the engine was embellished with carvings along the sides of the cab.

A letter published in the *Bridgewater Mercury* of October 1900 refers to *"unseemly pictures being exhibited"*.

In 1902 both Chipperfield's and Captain Rowland are reported as presenting shows featuring moving pictures. Rowland showed films of the coronation of King Edward and of local interest *"a run with the staghounds near Minehead"* Many showman with walk up variety shows added moving pictures as an added attraction. The travelling theatre was always dependent on novelty and the fairground showman was quick to add the latest

sensation to the shows. Some even combined wild beast shows with moving pictures, so as the flickering film finished half a dozen lions would suddenly appear on the stage. By the late 1890's all manner of fairground shows had to incorporate moving pictures to survive against the competition. Most of the films shown were of important national events such as the Diamond Jubilee of Queen Victoria, but many enterprising showman took films of local towns they were appearing in showing people going about their daily lives or taking part in sporting events. These proved to be particularly popular. W. C. & S. Hancock of Bristol presented a popular Bioscope at Bridgwater at the outbreak of the First World War. Marshall Hill and Anderton & Rowland also attended with the most lavish and elaborate Variety Theatres and Bioscope Shows for a similar period. Another showman who appeared regularly at Bridgwater was John Jones of Bristol who toured his "Empire" Show, a double fronted Bioscope which housed "Jones Circus Varieties". Jones began showing moving pictures in 1900. John Jones Empire last appeared at the fair in 1912.

The famous showman Hill Brothers had the distinction

Above: Onlookers admire Jones' 'Empire' Girls, paraders from the front of Jones' Cinematograph and Variety Show that attended Bridgwater Fair until 1912. *[Rosie Small]*

of presenting the last of the big elaborate Bioscope and parading shows at Bridgwater in 1913 when the chief attraction was the famous Wrestler Peter Gotz. The *Bridgwater Mercury* noted: *"As before mentioned there not as many large shows as usual Hill Bros. appeared to be the chief, the star turn of the programme being wrestling bouts by the well known Peter Gotz."* Most show proprietors went into the roundabout business and members of the Hill family and Anderton & Rowland attend the fair to this day.

The showman was the pioneer of the movie in the years before the permanent cinema took over. Fairground showmen such as Captain Rowland established cinemas in the West Country, opening the Empire Picture House in Torquay in 1922, and William Taylor built a cinema in his home town of Calne in Wiltshire.

The period from the 1880s to the 1939 was considered the hey-day of the great pleasure fair. The Hancocks, Hills, Heals and Anderton and Rowlands were among the showman who presented these lavish machines at Bridgwater. They became the backbone of the fair and were even more embellished with huge rounding boards and flamboyant marbled pillars giving an air of grandeur and opulence. The galloping horse was joined on the

roundabout by marvellously carved ostriches, cockerels, bears and even pigs. Stirring military marches blasted forth at great volume from the magnificent organ set in the centre of the ride. The innovation of pulsing coloured electric lights was a major draw for country dwellers. Electric lights arrived on the fairgrounds at the start of the 1890s. This was a huge improvement on the previously used naphtha lamps, which were dirty and on occasions proved to be hazardous. The power was provided by a portable engine. The Bioscope, the portable variety theatre and moving picture show, was the first to use electrical generators providing power not only for the lights, a great draw in themselves, but to power the bulky projector. From the 1880's the great Steam Switchback proved to be a great spectacle at the fair.

Until the start of the Great War the Bioscope Shows continued to appear at the fair along with the wonderfully lavish gilded Scenic railway such as the famous Golden Dragons with the huge organs in the centre appeared from the early 1920s joining the earlier Venetian Gondolas that had appeared from the turn of the century. The electric Scenic Railway was the next generation of faster lighter rides. They did not require a steam engine in the centre but were driven by electricity

Below: the Somerset swansong for the Bioscope show. 1913. James Hill presenting Marshall Hills Dreamland show featuring the famous wrestler of the day Peter Gotz as an added attraction to the films. *[Martin Burridge]*

generated from dynamos mounted on traction engines.

By now the pleasure section of the fair was beginning to overtake the livestock mart, although the agricultural side remained important for most of the 20th century. The *Bridgwater Independent* of fair week 1900 quotes an old Bridgwater saying *"Dry Weston fair wet Matthews fair"* and was true of the first year of the new century. But the storms during Wednesday evening did little to inconvenience the pleasure seekers. The reference to Weston is Westonzoyland, a village on the Somerset levels.

In 1901 Queen Victoria died on January 22nd after a reign lasting 64 years. The Biograph was noted as the most popular feature and scenes of the Queen's funeral were prominently featured. Other shows included performing birds, hares and reptiles *and a wonderful specimen of humanity from somewhere in the Fiji islands."* The teaser vendors did *"a roaring trade"*.

The Mercury of 1902 concludes, the business side of the fair has for many years dwindled in importance and is confined to a few hours on Wednesday morning. Although a popular annual event looked forward to by most of the townsfolk and those from the surrounding villages there have always been dissenting voices among the town's better off. The local press carried a selection of letters of complaint around the time of St Matthew's concerned with drunkenness, brawling, bad language, noise and disruption to trade and commerce. But in fact there is little evidence of bad behaviour or even drunkenness in the fair field and most news reports from the 1880s up until the outbreak of war in 1939 conclude by reporting good order being maintained for the duration of the fair. The commonest offence was pick pocketing.

In 1902 Marshall Hill's *"gorgeous switchback"* was the main feature of the fair along with two sets of Galloping Horse roundabouts, Captain Rowland's Moving pictures and Chipperfield's Electrograph and four smaller shows.

The *Independent* of 1904 reinforced the view that the fair is mainly given over to frivolity and fun: *"The Pleasure section of the fair has now became the most prominent part of the proceedings and the number of those who came who came into the town to participate in the fun must have created a record. They poured in by train and road from an early hour young and old alike being on pleasure bent. The 1904 St Matthews fair must be styled as the 'Bill Bailey' fair. The big switchback and roundabout organs pealed forth the plaintive air enquiring why the said William 'didn't come home'. There were some half dozen shows, the principle ones being Anderton & Rowland's variety entertainment and Chipperfield's animated pictures. There were two boxing booths and three large roundabouts, which together with the scenic railway did a roaring trade."*

A new innovation was introduced in 1905 the Big

Wheel, *"A contrivance which, if not as big as the monster which looms over Earls Court, yet affords wonderment and pleasure to its numerous patrons."* There were more shows than usual the principle ones being Anderton & Rowland's Empire Palace and Chipperfield's Show, both of which did a roaring trade. There were three boxing booths and a fat lady show.

In 1905 Anderton & Rowland's Grand Empire Palace lists their current programme of animated pictures on their advertising poster. They include the Great Riots in St Petersburg, the Great Strike in Paris, Mixed Bathing at Brighton, a Drama in the Air, and Historic Events during the reign of Louis X1V. As well as the pictures the show listed a 'grand variety' including conjuring by Professor Anderton, the Sisters May, vocalists, Cakewalkers and Skipping rope dancers, Charles Bruno the London Comedian with his latest songs and Miss Harvey in her beautiful serpentine dance. The poster concludes, *"We truly believe we are bringing to your town the grandest most elaborate Exhibition of its kind in Europe. An Empire Palace on Wheels! 2½ hours continuous. programme."* Prices ranged from 4d to 1s with children admitted at half price.

The *Bridgwater Mercury* carried a wonderful description of the fair in 1906 describing the Hancock's and Marshall Hill's Switchbacks but confirming that the main draw for the public was stills the travelling theatre. The early years of the 20th century were when the Bioscope show reached the height of its grandeur

Bridgwater Mercury

October 1906

This year the pleasure fair was on a more extensive scale than usual. The increase in the attractions bring largely due to the return after several years absence of Mr. Hancock, with his well known switchback and his Palace of Varieties. Hancock's and Marshall Hill's elaborate switchbacks and Heals Galloping Horses and Flying Ostriches occupied the centre of the field. But the chief allurement for the crowds consisted of Anderton and Rowland's handsomely fronted show. Chipperfields Variety Hall, Hancock s Palace of Varieties & Living Pictures and a large canvas building devoted to marionettes. The first named show was a veritable showman's triumph. The whole of the front was occupied with an intensely elaborate organ, and when at night this front was lit by varied coloured electric lamps the scene was entrancing in the extreme. Though it may seem unkind to say so, the exterior of these shows are more interesting than the interior, for the proceedings prior to filling the 'house' are more lengthy and attractive than the show itself, which usually consists of three living pictures and the thanks of the showman for the public's patronage. Not the least entertaining feature is the generous flow of superlative adjectives used by the show folk to accelerate entrance and the man times that the organ grinds out the National Anthem to give the impression that the entertainment is going to commence.

Around and about were other smaller shows, where for the payment of a small sum one could see 'the fattest girl on earth! — Many pounds heavier than the fat boy of Peckham!'; 'the smallest pony'; 'the largest Dane' and 'the smallest dog'~ and a war dance by a dejected looking Zulu who performed tricks with a weary monkey and two boa-constrictors. The sting of the latter, the showman, with a startling disregard for natural history, mentioned meant instant death. A tall-hatted, frock-coated Negro did good business with a conjuring entertainment (Prince Samouda), whilst there was also the usual boxing booth where local fighters had the opportunity of testing their skill with 'all the champions!'. Whilst Some were content to gaze, others tried their hand at the big wheel, coconut shies, shooting galleries, knocking clay pipes from the mouths of grinning tin coons, winning goldfish by pitching ping-pong balls into the glass bowls in which the diminutive little fish swam, skittles, covering a large red spot with small tin discs, throwing rings at the quoit board — sufficiently tipped to make the task well nigh impossible; knock down two out of three pins with a small ball, 'try your strengths' and 'photographs while you wait'. Most of these amusements seemed to be run either by impressively attired horoscopic professors, or else by dark-eyed. pretty faced Italian girls whose charm was apparently a valuable asset to the wrinkle-faced and soulless old proprietress standing close at hand. There were the smaller standings too, with their cheap-jacks. vendors of cockles, mussels and nougat, gingerbread and nuts, sellers of songs and Agapemone literature. In fact in every corner of the fair field had some queer little stall, presided over by a furtive-eyed, greasy looking gentlemen who continually informed his audience that for the performance of one simple trick the spectator could have 'any article on the stall', whilst others invited passers by to dip into a basket and 'whatever is marked on the ticket you have.' But unfortunately whilst the manager was loudly proclaiming "another concertina" the lady requires a large doll'', his obsequious attendant was regularly handing pins and pens to disappointed customers.

In the streets leading to the fair field stood gingerbread and sweet stalls, dispensers of quack remedies, retailers of cheap jewellery, aged and hoary headed minstrels, pavement artists, and the maimed, the halt and the blind seeking attention to their misfortunes. A plea enforced by the wail of an organette, as aged as their masters.

opulence and popularity peaking by 1907.

The account of the 1907 fair in the Independent reveals the scale of passenger traffic on fair day, claimed to be a record: G.W.R. Wednesday 3,700 passengers, Thursday 1,200. S. & D.J.R. Wednesday 800, Thursday 200. The town was served by the Great Western Railway and the Somerset and Dorset. Both companies had their own stations.

The pleasure fair consisted of Hancock's, Anderton & Rowland's and Jones' large shows, and lesser shows such as the Fattest Woman on Earth, two steam roundabouts, two steam switchback railways, a big wheel, a circular railway, three Helter Skelters, swinging boats, shooting galleries and numerous standings at which by performing a feat of skill one could have *"anything on the stall"*.

The arrangements for the fair were slightly different in 1908. The ground was laid out in two main avenues with the larger shows at the end. A circus occupied a different part of the fair field and the shows were Anderton and Rowland's handsomely fronted show, Hancock's well known variety show and Jones' hall of amusements. The main attraction though were two steam switchbacks and two steam roundabouts. Galloping horse roundabouts, according to Marshall Hill, had had their day. *"The Switchback has quite superseded the horses and I fear the popularity of the*

roundabout has gone for ever I attribute this to the fact that on the roundabout people are somewhat isolated but on the Switchback they can chum together," Mr Hill told the *Bridgwater Mercury* in 1909.

In 1909 Teasers, the water squirters with which young men had pursued young ladies with such gusto for many years, were officially banned by the Bridgwater Corporation and the outlawing of this pursuit was the talk of the town and divided opinion on the merits or otherwise of the ban. Although the teasers were banned the sale of confetti with which the boys also pursued the girls remained popular. The *Mercury* ran a large piece and interviewed the three leading showmen of the day, William Hancock, Captain Rowland and Marshall Hill. The showmen were instrumental in instigating a ban and the view of the corporation was that it lowered the tone and was responsible for keeping the *"better class people away from the fair, especially during the evening."* In fact Messrs. Anderton & Rowland were reported as having promoted a petition to the corporation in favour of the abolition of this peculiar phase of the fair, threatening that if teasing were permitted to continue they and other show folk would abstain from attending Bridgwater fair. The report of the 1908 fair hinted at the reason the showfolk were so against the boisterous pursuit. *"Teasing and confetti throwing was in the evening was pretty extensively enjoyed, and as usual*

Below: Marshall Hill's circular steam Switchback, built in 1896 after his partnership with William Symonds broke down because their wives could never agree on anything. *[Rod Fitzhugh]*

Above: Marshall Hill's Cake Walk and Switchback in 1910. *[Rod Fitzhugh]*

created a good deal of animosity between the showmen and the teaser vendors."

The firm of Anderton and Rowland suffered a tragedy on 5th August 1909 when the head of the family Albert Haslam (Professor Anderton) was found drowned in a brook at Sidmouth while the fair was open there. Just seven weeks later the family arrived at Bridgwater and Professor Anderton's son Captain Rowland, 37, was interviewed by the *Mercury* regarding his views on the ban on teasers. He maintained that *"orderliness was the making of a respectable fair and how can you* "he added *"have orderliness when you permit such scenes as take place at St. Matthews fair every night. Directly we light up there commences a perfect roar of teasers, and then the showman might just as well close his show. In every other fair from seven to ten are the showman's best hours, but at Bridgwater they are the worst. The people who come seem to go mad, and nothing else is thought of except the teasers. I have sometimes had many artistes outside my show to try and stay the people, but no, they rush about with the teasers and take no notice of anything. I think the corporation's action is a splendid one and it will be the making of the fair. In no other fairs I attend are such nuisances permitted and why should they be allowed at Bridgwater? Last year we show people made up our mind that we would shun Bridgwater if the abominable teasers were not stopped, and after all it is us who make the fair and not the teasers."*

William Hancock, a more experienced showman at 55, was however of the same opinion: *"It will be the making of the fair. At present respectable people will not come to the fair in the evening. You may take it from me, that at no other chartered fair in Great Britain is such a thing allowed."* When asked how long he had been attending Bridgwater fair Mr Hancock replied *"Over forty years. When I came to Bridgwater first I had only a little roundabout that I had to push around by hand, but I have moved on."* The interviewer remarked that, *"Some people seem to imagine you make a larger amount of money from the fair."* *"Do they?"* replied Mr Hancock cynically. *"Let 'em try the business! They forget the expense of running such a concern. Look at the capital embodied in our shows. One of the Switchbacks represents at least £4,000, and then there is the ground on which you stand to rent. There are the railway rates and wages of the men and we employ over fifty. When you come to think it over you see it is not all profit."*

Marshall   Hill, 43, and   vice president of the Showmen's Guild also expressed an opinion on the ban. *"I think that the corporation's act is a very good thing, but I quite appreciate that there is a sharp division of opinion in the town. Probably the working classes are in favour of the teasers and the better class against. But you cant make a fair by catering solely for the working class. Mind you, I am not saying a word against the working class, but to make a good fair you need to attract the presence of the better class as well. Unlike some showman I travel in eighteen to twenty counties and I must say it is the only big fair where teasers are allowed in this part of the country. There will be a great improvement in the character of Bridgwater fair if the teasers are abolished and you will find a better class of people coming. To be frank I don't think the teasers interfere with my business but they make a great deal of difference to people who have shows. I don't say there is anything wrong or immoral about teasing, but as I pointed out to the Mayor last year, when respectable people see four or five young fellows rush after a girl and drown her with water from the teasers then plaster her in confetti, naturally such a person is apt to say 'This is not the sort of place to bring my wife or daughter.'*

The vendors who made a considerable profit from their annual sale also made their views on the ban clear in the same newspaper report. Jeffrey Gillingham of Bridgwater who was described as the leader of the teaser fraternity and who had sold teasers for the past sixteen years said, *"Teasers have been sold at the fair the last thirty years and the bulk of those who patronise the fair would not come if they knew of the teaser ban. It is all*

very well for the show people to talk about getting a better class of people to the fair, but who is it, I would like to know, who patronise the shows? It is the working class and not the toffs!"

As well as the combined attractions of Hancock's, Hill Brothers and Anderton and Rowland's, Hodgini's Mexican Circus played to full houses each day and evening that year.

As the Edwardian era drew to a close in 1910 following the king's death in May of that year, it also marked the beginning of the demise of the grand Bioscope show. As taste and choice in entertainment moved on at a great pace, by the start of the Great War in 1914 the Bioscopes had virtually disappeared.

By 1910 Bridgwater had its own permanent cinema, the Bijou, in St Mary Street.

Speeding traction engine drivers were the focus of attention for the town's constabulary in 1910 when four drivers were found guilty of exceeding the 2 miles per hour speed limit introduced by Act of Parliament in 1865. Gilbert Anderton, show proprietor, was charged with driving at three miles an hour. Mr. Anderton told the bench that he had driven all over England and Wales and had never been summonsed previously. He was fined 5s. and costs. At the same sitting, presided over by the Mayor, William Eddy, an engine driver in the

Below: Anderton & Rowland's Burrell engine *Admiral Beresford* with the cinematograph show. *[DeVey family]*

34

Above: Marshall, Bernard and Ernest Hill, with family and staff, on the Scenic Railway in 1914. *[Brian Wells]*

employment of Mr. Jones, show proprietor of Bristol, was charged with a similar offence. William Platz, an engine driver employed by Mr. Pruett, roundabout proprietor, was fined the same amount. During the same week an application was made to the bench for a licence to permit a ten year old girl to perform inside Messrs. Hancock's show. The girl's mother, stage name Lilly Voelker, stated that her daughter really had nothing to do other than be put into a sack on the stage. Neither the girl nor her mother had been used to this sort of work before being Music Hall artistes. The bench granted the licence for Thursday and Friday from noon till 9.00 pm.

The *Independent* gives a detailed account of the fair in 1910 when it was in a state of transition from the attractions from being mainly big shows to being dominated by roundabouts: *"The end of the ground was occupied by Messrs. Anderton & Rowland's and Hancock's handsomely fronted shows, both of the performances in both consisted mainly of animated pictures, interspersed with variety turns by artistes.*

Each of the shows was well patronised although it must be confessed that generally, the better performance took place on the outside prior to the commencement of the entertainments. Jones theatre also proved a popular resort and other places of amusement included a clever exhibition of swimming under water, 'the smallest people on earth', two boxing booths and a stereoscopic exhibition. The greatest attraction at the fair was probably the steam-propelled roundabouts and

switchbacks of which there were four throughout the fair these revolving affairs were crowded with passengers. Indeed so liberal was public patronage that the proprietor of one of the switchbacks confessed that it was the best financial return he had enjoyed from St. Matthew's Fair for five years. Each roundabout and switchback was fitted with an elaborate and costly electrophone as, indeed, were many of the shows, and as each was accustomed to play a different popular air at the same time the din was such as only an English fair can produce. The scene at dusk, when the shows were brilliantly illuminated by electric arc lights was quite fascinating. The illumination by electricity of the standings as well as shows seems to be spreading, and one almost shudders to apprehend the time when the venerable cocoanut [sic] of one youth will be illuminated by the gleam of the arc light rather than the flare of the homely naphtha lamp".

In fact 1910 was the last year that W. C. & S. Hancock's Show appeared at the fair. The Mercury notes its absence in the account of the 1911 fair: "The most popular attractions are undoubtedly the Roundabouts, of which there were five, two of the Switchback class and three of the ordinary horse character. Messrs. M and E. Hill's "Scenic Railway" an elaboration on the Switchback type, was the most gorgeous, but the other roundabouts also claimed a good share of patronage .There were two "Joy Wheels", and these novel forms of amusement caused a good deal of fun, and the twirling sensation appeared to be much

Above: Marshall Hill's Scenic Railway and Whitelegg's Helter Skelter.

enjoyed. There was also a Cake Walk. There were not as many shows as usual; Messrs. Hancock's well known variety theatre being absent this year. Anderton & Rowland's and Jones both did good business, as also did the two boxing booths, Mr. Alf Wright of Bristol, who ran one exhibition of the noble art, kindly interested himself on behalf of the widow of an engine driver named Gilbert who was killed last week in Bridgwater under most distressing circumstances. He made a collection among the showfolk and among those who patronised his booth and he was enabled to hand over £3.4s.1d. to the fund. Other side shows included a clever model of a coal mine, an exhibition of tiny people and turns by a strong lady. There was the usual array of coconut Shies, try your strength and shooting galleries. The game of houp-la was very much in evidence, but it seems to be losing its popularity. In the evenings the fair was brilliantly illuminated by the flare of many powerful arc lamps and the homely flare of naphtha lamps was very fascinating, and with the music from the many ornate organs the proceedings were indeed cheery. The ban on 'teasers' being continued by the Corporation the fun of the fair was again supplied by confetti, huge quantities of which were sold to the merry men and maidens, who derived plenty of fun in scattering paper

particles over one and other. It is pleasing to note that during the fair excellent order was maintained under the direction of the Chief Constable Mr W.J. Davey the police force carried out its duties admirably, the display of tact and ability most marked."

The paper went on to report on a sequel to a football match between the employees of two show proprietors, Anderton & Rowland and M. & B. Hill. The match was held on the Malt Shovel Field, just a short distance from the fair field and during the game an opportunist thief stole a gold watch chain belonging to the pianist on Anderton's Show, one Sidney William. The Bridgwater police soon recovered the chain and apprehended the thief, a stranger to the town named Henry Hall, who was arrested at his lodgings in West Street. P.S Slocombe of the Bridgwater police must have been a particularly diligent officer as his name appears often in the court columns for this period.

The writing was on the wall for the Bioscope shows as Bridgwater's new Bijou cinema showed its first animated picture during fair week of 1910. By 1912 Hancock's great show was offered for sale and in the same year Anderton & Rowland's ceased to operate their show. By then both firms had moved into the business of roundabout proprietors. The last show of its

36

type to visit was John Jones Empire Show which last appeared in 1912. The Palace Theatre in Penel Orlieu opened in 1916 at first as a theatre but it soon converted to a cinema. This handsome building with its distinctive dome fell in to dereliction for many years but is now a thriving night club. By 1912 there were 4,000 licensed cinemas in the country and soon after the big business men and theatre tycoons began to build up empires of cinema chains that controlled the majority of the business and were squeezing out the independent operators. But there is no doubt that the explosion in the popularity of cinema was a direct result of the fledgling industry being pioneered and persevered with by fairground showmen. Ironically it was the permanent cinema which became the main competition for the fairground prior to the widespread ownership of televisions after the Second World War.

The *Mercury* report of the 1912 fair stated that, *"in point of size and variety 1912 constituted a record, the oldest residents failing to recall a time when there were more shows and forms of amusements. Practically the whole space allocated to the amusements was taken up and on the whole they had a profitable time. The field was divided into two main avenues and contained the usual varied amusements. The far end was occupied by the roundabouts and large shows, and the sides of the avenues with the miscellaneous standings. West Street is*

especially a favoured pitch by those who desire the patronage of good nature of the Britsher out for fun. The maimed and blind were present in abundance ,calling attention to their calamities, whilst itinerant musicians of great variety sought the generosity of passers by ventriloquists, conjurors, acrobats, Punch & Judy and dancers were busy on route to the fair, whilst the raucous voices of the cheap–jacks and herbalist doctors resounded from every point of vantage. The bulk of stalls here being devoted to the sale of vegetables and for the outlay of a copper the reveller could be regaled with a varied course including steaming faggots, hot chips, fried fish and Bombay cockles and last but not least nougat. The latter is always popular."

"The chief part of the fair is shows and roundabouts. There were two horse roundabouts, two switchbacks and a scenic railway .Another form of roundabout was the American Flip Flap, the motion of which was distinctly peculiar. The sensation was said by some to be pleasing and others it was reminiscent of a squally day at sea. Another innovation was the Semi-Twister and judging by the risibility which it created among those who ventured in the grotesquely jerking car its presence was appreciated. There were also two Joy Wheels. The shows were more numerous than in some years the chief being Anderton & Rowland, Kemp & Son [actually Marshall Hill who purchased the show from Kemp] and

Above: Looking through the Switchback towards the Galloping Horses. Gratton's Boxing Booth can be seen in the show line of this 1915 shot of the busy war time fair.

Chipperfield. At each moving pictures were the chief item of the programme. A variety of subjects were dealt with in the lesser shows such as Snake charming a mini menagerie, the smallest pony etc and animal freaks."

In the 1913 account of the fair, as usual diligently reported upon by the local press, the fact that the two large shows of Hancocks and Andertons are absent is lamented by the writer. *"The pleasure side was hardly as extensive as last year. The absence of one or two well known showman was mainly responsible for the diminishment. The end of the two avenues of the field suffered the greater by their failure to visit the town, one missing the gorgeous fronts of their theatres."* The writer was under the impression that the showman had given Bridgwater a miss in 1913. The sad fact was that both large shows had been taken off the road by their proprietors as a result of a falling-off of revenue due almost entirely to the boom in permanent cinemas, and moving pictures were no longer a novelty. Had the reporter taken the trouble to seek out Billy Hancock and Captain Rowland and brothers, he would no doubt have been given a full and frank report on the reasons for bringing the curtain down for the final time.

Both showman were at the fair that year presenting steam roundabouts. The demise of the large walk up shows left room for the novelty or side show exhibition to flourish for the period up to the 1960s.

The only large show in 1913 was presented by Marshall Hill, who ironically had hitherto been a roundabout proprietor. He purchased the elaborate Dreamland show from George Kemp in 1911. Marshall Hill's eldest son, James, travelled the show around the West Country for two years. Jim Hill married Mary, a parader on the show.

In 1914 the platform of Marshall Hill's show was used to appeal for recruits to Kitchener's Army. Jim Hill along with his brother joined up and the show was put into storage and never returned to the fairgrounds. Colonel Patton, addressing the crowds said the army required young men who had been in the habit of riding and accustomed to the care of horses. He believed there a great many of that class at the fair and he believed many of them would respond to their country's call.

The fair was reduced in size that year the principal attraction being Marshall Hill's Show, which showed pictures of Belgian war scenes, several menageries, a fat lady and a tent which exhibited 'living statuary', two boxing booths (Wright's and Gratton's) and several conjuring and telepathic exhibitions. Marshall Hill's

sons had already joined up and were on leave from the Army. The *Mercury* describes the amusements as being comprised *"Several roundabouts and Switchbacks, two cycle merry go rounds a cake walk and a Helter Skelter the evening there were merry scenes with confetti, but on the whole, there was ever the grim shadow of war. By order of the justices the licensed booths the sale of intoxicating liquor were closed an hour earlier than usual."*

During the First World War the fair was on a smaller scale with the public mood being understandably subdued. In 1916 there was only one show, Prince Samouda, 'The man of a thousand mysteries'. Prince Samouda was a very successful conjuror and showman. He also developed a business supplying tricks and props he had invented. Samouda commenced his presentation of conjuring on the fairgrounds in 1896 and was an immediate favourite with the public. He graduated to working in theatre both in this country and on the continent and claimed to have worked for James Bailey. the partner of the great American showman Barnum. He was engaged by the theatrical impresario Sir Edward Moss at his theatres in London and Edinburgh in 1906.

PRINCE SAMOUDA

19 years ago.
Past Mark-Master of Oriental Wonder Workers.

In 1916 there were four large roundabouts from M. & B. Hill and Anderton & Rowland. Lighting restrictions were imposed for the duration and fair closed at 8 p.m. each evening. The following year arrangements were made for the fair to remain open until later but the lights had to be subdued. Bright moonlight meant the fair was able to stay open until 10 p.m. Several showfolk fell foul of the lighting restrictions and the ever vigilant Bridgwater policeman. Charlotte Whitelegg was summonsed for having a flare lamp lit on her stall at 8.45. Florence Harrison of Bedminster was summonsed for a similar offence. Both were fined 10 shillings. During the same week James Cole, travelling showman, was summonsed for leading a grey mare without a lamp being carried and fined 7s 6d.

The Great War which ended in 1918 had an effect on the fair and business was further hampered by the railwayman's strike that year. Dealers were unable to attend and the bulk of the showman's equipment was dependent on rail travel at that time. The pleasure fair in 1918 was the smallest on record and the Corporation lost between £40 and £50 in tolls as a result of the rail strike. Only one Scenic Railway was in attendance and the smaller show stuff which travelled by road were reported to have enjoyed good business.

Between the Wars

Above: The inscription on the back of this post card reads *"The outdoor service team, Uncle Fred with the megaphone."* [Rod Fitzhugh Collection]

In 1919 the West Country economy experienced something of a boom as agricultural prices and wages rose and a bumper fair was recorded. Among the commodities enjoying good sales were cheeses, fruit and vegetables and cloth. The pleasure fair was laid out by the borough surveyor in three avenues as opposed to the previous two and congestion was avoided even though the crowds were greater. Sideshows included the 'Heaviest Girl in the World', the 'Women of Mystery', the 'Man Sea Lion', 'La Blanche, the Beautiful Artists Model', performing birds and assorted freaks of nature.

There were two Boxing Pavilions where the noble art was practised, and several local men took part including Sergt. C. Wilcox, D.C.M. Other attractions included a Switchback, two Galloping Horse roundabouts, Cycle merry go round, Helter Skelter and a Wiggle Woggle. On both days evangelistic services were held in West Street, Nonconformist ministers taking part, while the Salvation Army held services in the same street.

At the 1920 fair a lady lion tamer appeared on the show line along with a 'Bush-Baby from East Africa', Gratton's boxing booth, a fat lady and a circus, although the field was dominated by Anderton & Rowlands Gondolas, a Scenic Railway, two sets of Galloping

Horses and a Helter Skelter. The *Independent* noted that *"over £300 was raised in tolls from the pleasure fair."*

A generous offer was made by the showman at the 1921 Fair to give up some of their takings for the War memorial fund...The period was from 6.00 to 6.30 on the Friday evening and the amount realised was £10.11s.11d, the contributions being Golden Dragons (Anderton & Rowland) £4.4s; Electric Motors (Marshall Hill) £2.7s; The Gallopers (Charles Heal) £1.15s 6d; ditto (Ernest Hill) £1.1s.6d; Helter Skelter (Harry Coneley) 11s; Joy Wheel (W. Jones) 7s 3d; Cake Walk (James Hill) 4s 2d. Many showmen operating at the fair had served in the War, including the Hill Brothers and Billy Butlin, who served in the Canadian Army in Flanders.

Anderton & Rowland's electric Golden Dragon scenic railway was one of the most famous and popular roundabouts ever to grace the fairgrounds of the West Country and visited Bridgwater until it was converted to the Diving Dolphin in 1936. The machine was delivered by rail to Newton Abbot earlier in the year but the final decorative work arrived from makers, Messrs Orton, Sons and Spooner's works in Burton upon Trent, and were fitted in time for the fair.

Above: Billy Jones' Joy Wheel. *[Rosie Small]* *Below:* Thomas Whitelegg's F.W.D. lorry. *[Nigel Burt]*

Above: Anderton & Rowland's Golden Dragons. *[DeVey Family]*

The *Mercury* describes their debut in 1921: *"The chief attraction was the Golden Dragons switchback of Anderton & Rowland's with its fine organ, scenic effects and charming waterfall. The Golden Dragons were the most popular feature on the field the cars were always crowded with pleasure seekers. Among the human and animal oddities exhibited that year was Emma the Pig Faced Girl, the Limbless Lady, the Human Spider, two fat girls, a four-legged cockerel and a giant rat "captured by British troops in the trenches". The tolls received from the pleasure fair were £313 as against £316 in 1920."*

In the mid 1920s FWD Lorries, mainly ex-Army, were used for lighter loads but the mighty showman's traction engines made by Burrells, Fowlers, Garrett and Wallis & Stevens provided the main means of both hauling the equipment loads and also powering the rides and producing electricity to drive the lights. Before the war horses were used. Large numbers of horses could be seen grazing in fields surrounding the fair at this time. It took as many as sixteen horses to haul some loads. To climb steep West Country hills the showmen used to pool their horses to get loads to the top.

The Bristol based showman, Marshall Hill, one of the most prominent in the country and one time vice president of the Showman's Guild had a fleet of engines with patriotic names such as *Vanguard, King George V, Hercules,* and *Bristol City,* while Anderton & Rowland had an equally impressive fleet. In the early 1920s the firm used *Lord Nelson, The Gladiator,* and *Earl Beatty.* Another well known engine at Bridgwater was the Burrell *Prince of Wales* owned by Harry Coneley, which provided light for his Helter Skelter in its blaze of light, standing like a sentry over the whole fair. Somerset's best known showman Charlie Heal, whose family originated from Glastonbury, was proud of his fleet which included the Burrells *His Majesty* and *Bristol City.*

By 1922 the fair had grown again and more space in St Matthew's Field was allocated to the pleasure fair. Among the showmen present were Anderton & Rowland, Marshall Hill, Ernest Hill, Bernard Hill, Geo Hill, Jim Hill, Charles Heal, Messrs. Harrison and Son and Harry Coneley. The *Mercury* reported that a new feature of the fair was the Chair-o-Planes, of which four were present. These were generally of German manufacturer. Fred Stock of Bailey Street fell from one of the Chair-o-Planes at about 9 o'clock on Thursday, and was rendered unconscious. He soon recovered and was able to proceed home. In addition to the Golden Dragons Scenic railway two lots of "horses", two Joy Wheels, a Cakewalk, Helter Skelter, Mountain Glide, Temple of Mirth, Sam McKeowen's Boxing Booth and the usual fat lady was Elsie Hopton, 15 years old and weighing nearly 30 stone. A new show, Limehouse by Night, was described as *"a playlet, exposing the opium and cocaine habits"* Described by its exhibitor as *"the strangest freak of nature ever exhibited"* was Ursa, the

41

Bear Lady. Another side show was the 'Mysterious She'.

The *Bridgwater Mercury* reported the increase in size of the 1923 fair: *"The Pleasure Fair was of greater extent than in recent years. The field ably planned by Borough Engineer F. Parr. Well known Amusement caterers such as Anderton & Rowland, Hills, Harrisons, Coneleys, Jones, Heals and others had a lot to do with the making of the fair. There were four large Roundabouts and three lots of Chair-o-Planes all of which were extensively patronised. Other attractions included a Mountain Glide [Jim Hill], Helter Skelter [H. Coneley] and two Cakewalks [Anderton & Rowland and Jim Hill]. There were a considerable number of Houp-las and these provided an enormous attraction particularly those that adopted a popular Aeroplane game. Boxing Booths run by Alf Wright and Jack Lemm drew crowded houses, another booth had Wrestlers. Sideshows included a Menagerie, Mrs Tom Thumb, a Dusky Prince and Princess. A show which of much attraction was a cleverly designed and electrically driven working model of a convict prison. West Street had its share of standings and cheapjacks. The latter claimed to there only for the benefit of the public, but the fact that many of them possessed motor cars or vans was evidence that there was a huge profit somewhere."*

The *World's Fair* account fills in the detail of the attractions as Paulo's Circus, Harvey's Mystery Show

Above: Advertising Card for Ursa the Bear Lady who appeared at Bridgwater in the 1920s.

Below: Marshall Hill's Bristol showman's engine *Bristol City* with his Circular Steam Switchback.

Above: Building up Harrison's Chair-o-Planes at Bridgwater in the 1920s. *[Rod Fitzhugh]*

Above: Building up the Chair-o-Planes for the 1924 fair, with Heal's and Anderton & Rowland's 4-abreast Gallopers in the background. *[Rod Fitzhugh]*

other shows by Lennards, Stockwells and T. Keyes, shooters by John Gratton and Jones. The four roundabouts referred to in the *Mercury* were the 4-abreast Gallopers Anderton & Rowland and Charles Heal, Anderton & Rowland's Golden Dragons and M. Hill's Scenic Railway.

The following year the fair was reported to have been *"larger than for some years and attracted visitors from Bristol, Taunton, Yeovil and Glastonbury on special rail excursions."* There were no less than five large roundabouts which proved as popular as ever as well as Chair-o-Planes, Cakewalks, a Mountain glide, Helter Skelter and numerous other attractions. There were a number of small shows mainly of the freak type, two boxing booths attracted many to *"the noble art"*. A great attraction for the many townsfolk and indeed those from surrounding villages in 1925 was skittling for the chance to win a motor car, the value of which was £400. The game of skittles was and remains a popular pastime in the town and no doubt this proved a great attraction. The plethora of rides on offer that year comprised Marshall Hill's Scenic Railway, Harry Coneley's Helter Skelter, Richard's Razzle Dazzle Hill's, Anderton & Rowland's and Nash's Cake Walks, Anderton's famous Golden Dragons and three magnificent Galloping Horse

roundabouts provided by Charles Heal, Ernest Hill and Anderton & Rowland, as well as Jones's Chair Planes. Of special note was a telepathic musical display presented by De Alba in which the gifted lady played pieces of music the audience was thinking of. This was a very popular Music Hall act at the time. Anderton & Rowland placed an advert in the Somerset County Gazette directing the public's attention to the Golden Dragons Scenic Railway, *"the finest machine in Great Britain. All should hear the Grand Organ playing the world's best music. The Waterfall is well worth seeing, decorated with hundreds of fairy lights."*

An eye witness account of the 1926 fair reveals that the grand family rides were the main feature, the Cinematograph and large Bioscope show having been consigned to history after the Great War. The attractions included Anderton & Rowland's Golden Dragons Scenic, 4-abreast Gallopers and Chair-o-Planes, Charles Heal's 4-abreast, the late Marshall Hill's Motor Car Scenic, the late Ernest Hill's 4-aBreast, Hill's Cakewalk, H. Jones Chair-o-Planes, Lennard's Jolly Tubes and the late Harry Coneley's and Tom Whitelegg's Helter Skelters. Shows included McKeowen's Spider Illusion, and Boxing, Jim Style's Variety and Freak Shows, Shuflebottom's Wild West,

44

Big Chief Red Snakes Conjuring Show Len Smith's Freaks, Wheatley's Midgets, *Dunlop* the India Rubber man and *Andy* the Sea-lion-man. Heavy rain made the going tough for the showmen in 1927 and the Bridgwater Mercury reports,

In 1928 there were reported to be five large roundabouts including the Diving Dolphins three lots of Galloping Horses and one Switchback Railway. There was a Helter Skelter, two Cake Walks, two sets of Jolly Tubes, Chair-o-planes and an American Joy Ride. The Joy ride was a an amusement device, although common in the rest of the country, not before seen in the West: a set of Steam Yachts. They were owned by the Yorkshire-based Waddingtons, who travelled with Anderton & Rowland's for the back end run of 1928. Other shows included two boxing booths and two circuses, the 'woman they told lies about: London's Largest Lass', the Cabaret Girls and the Wonders of the World Show, said to include the smallest horse and smallest bull in the world, a lamb with six legs a chicken with four legs and a hare with two bodies and eight legs.

1929 saw the most popular and enduring of all fairground rides first appear at Bridgwater. The Dodgems were an American invention, first known as Auto Skooters or Radio cars. The first set was presented by E.W Hill & Son's of Bristol. Tremendous patronage was also recorded on the famous Golden Dragons. There were three sets of Galloping Horses. The following year

Below: Anderton & Rowland's Burrell *Queen Mary* which worked with their Dodgem track. *[DeVey family]*

45

there were two Dodgem tracks, as well as three Galloping Horse roundabouts, the Golden Dragons, Chair-o-Planes, Cake Walk and a new sensation-the Lightning Swirl.

The *Mercury* of October 1929 comments on the latest fairground sensation: *"A new feature in Bridgwater caught on immensely, the continuous collisions between motor cars arousing shrieks of laughter from the joy-riders and causing much amusement to onlookers."* In fact so successful were the Dodgems received in the town that Mr Hill returned to Bridgwater in June the following year to present his 'Great Fun City' at Bridgwater Albion Football Field and placed a large advert in the *Independent* inviting patrons to *"Come and see the New Dodgem Cars"*. Other attractions were his 4-abreast Gallopers and other side shows

The Dodgem was introduced to this country in 1928 by a West Country showman who had appeared regularly at the fair, Billy Butlin. In 1921 Butlin attended the fair with a single stall he made himself and travelled by train, by 1926 he had five lorries, employed 53 men and had 5 Spinner stalls and 150 feet of side stalls. He also had Racing Spiders, Stop the Clock and the Kentucky Derby game. His staff wore smart uniforms with jackets with a letter *B* on the front. The uniform trousers were made without pockets or turn ups to lessen the risk of *fiddling* with the takings. Butlin became one of the most famous showmen of his generation building at first a chain of amusement parks and later his famous holiday camp empire. He was later knighted for his charity work. Butlin was a nephew of Marshall Hill and based in Bedminster and he travelled the western fair circuit starting out in the spring at Axbridge and finishing off the season at Bridgwater.

Hard on the heels of the Dodgems came the Noah's Ark, an attraction which first appeared in Germany but was soon being manufactured in large numbers in Britain and remained popular until the end of the 1970s. A fast undulating circular ride on which riders sat on wooden animals.

There was anxiety expressed in the showman's paper, the *World's Fair*, in April 1930 regarding proposed changes by the borough to St Matthew's Field following its purchase. In a report of a recent council meeting the subject was raised. Parts of the field were owned by different people but eventually all the parcels of land came under the ownership of the Corporation. Councillor Webber, referring to the proposed new layout, said he understood the principal reason for the purchase of St. Matthew's Field was for the layout of St Matthew's Fair but nothing was mentioned in the minutes of the last council meeting. Alderman Dobson replied that that it [the new layout] was being considered in detail; they wanted to get a tentative scheme. Councillor Chard said that *"it had got into people's minds that the fair would be done away with."* Alderman Dobson said the prime objective of the purchase of the field was to provide better facilities for the fair. The fair had been a quagmire; indeed certain parts of the field were used to grow potatoes and these were only harvested a few days prior to the arrival of the showman. The potato patch days were over for now, but part of the field, where the sheep were penned, was once again used to grow crops during the Second World War. Proposed developments included the provision of two football pitches, a large playground, roadways, fencing off the allotments and public conveniences. After 1930 the field was considerably improved which led to the rapid growth of the fair over the next decade.

As well as the rent from the showmen, agricultural dealers and other traders at St. Matthew's Fair, the council has had since 1930 a regular income from letting part of the field to Circuses. Such famous shows as Bertram Mills', Chipperfield's and Sir Robert Fossett's have all held performances on the field.

Two small walk up Circuses appeared in 1930: the ever popular Chipperfield's and Paulo's, both of these shows had West County roots. Chipperfield's was a firm favourite in the town and Ricardo as Richard Chipperfield was known would persuade a couple of ladies from the crowd to join him in the Lions cage. Their reward for this brave deed was a box of chocolates and some publicity in the local press. The 1930 fair featured three sensational new motorcycle displays, the Wall of Death, the Globe of Death and the Wall Wizards. The thrilling Wall became a firm favourite at Bridgwater until the early 1980s. Charles Heal's 4-abreast Gallopers and Dodgems were also prominent among the attractions. It was reported that a visitor who died suddenly while at the fair remained unidentified at the inquest a week later. The tolls from the pleasure fair were a record amount of £415, up £35 on the previous year.

From the late 1920s thrills of another kind were offered by posing or 'Tableaux Vivants.' Naked or partially clothed women could be legally exhibited (there was often a legal challenge by the police or watch committees) in the name of art. The performers were not permitted to move or an offence had been committed. The one that visited Bridgwater was billed as Yvonne, the 'Rage of Paris' and a banner proclaimed *'The Perfect Venus, Living Art Studies, Living Statuary'.* The showman would have left no doubt in the punters' mind at what was on offer. The admission charge in the late 1920s was 3d in the day time, but the ticket was 'flipped' to 6d after dark. These were the forerunners of

Below: Charles Heal's 4-abreast Gallopers. *[Rod Fitzhugh]*

Above: Yvonne, the Rage of Paris. *[DeVey family]*

the late 1930s striptease show which were a regular fixture in various guises until disappearing in the late 1970s.

Rumours were rife that the 1931 fair would not take place as the result of discussions between the Borough and the Showman's Guild over the thorny matter of the rent being levied. The *Independent* reported that the matter had been resolved for the current year and the age old event would, after all, take place as usual. The question of banning confetti, another of the showmen's grievances, was raised at a council meeting in September. It disrupted the business in the evening and the Guild pressed for its banning.

By 1932 the financial depression was starting to affect the spending power of the residents of Somerset. The *World's Fair* reported: *"The same amusements were there, but money did not flow as freely as in other years. Seven big rides were present as well as children's roundabouts and two Helter Skelters and swing boats. Messrs. Anderton & Rowland bought their magnificent Diving Dolphins under the command of George DeVey. The Jungle Ride captained by Ernest DeVey and the Dodgem track under the control of Nelson DeVey. Then there was Charles Heal's Dodgems and good old fashioned four-abreast Galloping Horses. All the horses*

looked in the pink of condition and many were the riders. Also present was Hill Brothers' magnificent Noah's Ark ride ablaze with amber coloured lights. I noticed a lot of the joints are using coloured lights and they look all the better for the fairy like radiance. Next to the Ark was Harry Coneley's Dodgem. All three Dodgem tracks had a comic figure wobbling about on it. Then there was the weird Ghost Train of Hill Bros two imposing edifices: the Helter Skelter of John Butlin and the Alpine Glide of Tom Whitelegg." *"Foremost among the shows and the biggest was the Royal Empire Circus with its fine show front. The talented company under the direction of Mr John Fossett remains the same and they give a great little show. Miss Rosie Purchase dances inside the Lion's den in Chipperfield's show, as well as doing a snake charming act. The trainer also makes a Bengal tiger perform tricks. Next was Joe Silverstone's Autodrome of Death. Another good show was the Hippodrome of Varieties with Mr Len Smith presenting Big Chief Red Snake assisted by his American wonder girls and their miracle show. Big Chief Red Snake makes a very imposing figure in his large feathered headdress and Indian costume and is very adept at sleight of hand, making eggs vanish and re appear like lightning. Miss Chiquita and Miss Brenda* assist him in the mysterious sack trick in which Brenda is enclosed in a sack which is securely tied by a gentleman from the audience and a few seconds alter emerges from the sack, leaving it still tied. Len Smith was from Warminster in Wiltshire and ran a succession of small shows known as Pony Circuses over the years. Two boxing booths put on great sporting performances, Sam McKeowen's famous academy and that of Tim Sullivan of South Wales."

"The other big show was the Globe of Death. The performers Charles, Sidney and Nadine Abbin so well-known in England and on the continent. They ride around inside a circular ball of iron lattice work, riding all around and looping the loop. It is a wonderful show run by Hill Brothers. There was also a small Circus run by Hill Brothers. Next to this little show was the fattest Schoolgirl and schoolboy. These two are a buxom pair as it has ever been my lot to see. The girl who is a real giantess is aged 16 and was born in Torquay; the boy, who is a tremendous size is also 16 and comes from Norfolk. There is also the famous showman Mr James R Styles with his novelty shows Titania the fat girl and Kana the midget and his miniature zoo. I noticed the boys and girls of the Harrison family looking extremely smart in white coats with blue collars and cuffs. How much smarter a joint looks when those in charge of it are in uniform."

The *Bridgwater Mercury* gives an insight in to the

1933 event : "Old Time Festival Comes Round Again. About 6,000 Sheep and Lambs. Extensive Pleasure Fair: St. Matthews business and pleasure fair which has a history going back over many centuries, opened at Bridgwater last Wednesday, as in previous years. The main thoroughfares were thronged with people as the visitors wended their way to the fairground at the top of West Street. Crowds poured into the town by road and rail, but it is generally acknowledged that the streets were not as thickly populated as is usually the case on the first day. As is generally the case the sheep auctions were confined to the first day and it opened shortly after 10 o'clock. The pleasure seeking public flocked to the fairground in as great as numbers as ever and revelled in the wide range of attractions the amusement caterers had provided for them. The fair was spread over a large area being well up to the average regarding the site. And been well planned by the borough engineer, leaving plenty of room for the crowds to move about in comfort. Many new and varied forms of entertainment enabled these people whom the fair makes an appeal to enjoy themselves to the full. As popular as ever were the large handsome roundabouts with their powerful organs playing popular tunes but one missed Messrs. Anderton & Rowland's Golden Dragons, which have been at the fair for a number of years. Instead they provided a new form of entertainment in the way of the Lightning Swirl, an attraction which did an enormous amount of

Below: T. Whitelegg's Dodgems. [Whitelegg/Shepeard Collection]

49

Above: Whitelegg's Burrell engine, *Dreadnought,* working with the Waltzer. *[Cecil Quick]*

business. There was one set of Galloping Horses and three sets of Dodgems then there were two Noah's Arks and a Wall of Death. The proprietors of the latter invited local young ladies to ride pillion around the wall and several members of the fair sex experienced this novel form of thrill. Mr Geoffrey Gillingham of Bridgwater catered for the kiddies with his Merry Go Round. The Ghost Train drew the usual popular patronage and there were also Switchbacks, a Helter Skelter, touchems and innumerable shooting galleries, coconut shies and other amusements all added to all the fun of the fair. Chipperfield's Menagerie in which Miss Kate Purchase, daughter of the late Capt. Purchase entered the cage of Lions drew a very large crowd. Two boxing booths provided entertainment for devotees of the noble art. There were an usually large number of small shows containing a variety of attractions. Those wishing to try their skill were enabled to do so by patronising the many stalls into which they had to roll pennies into squares, and stalls laden with prizes, whereby the lucky ticket holders could select their own choices were once again, largely patronised. There were stalls for the sale of sweets and gingerbread and cups of tea and their four licensed tents for the sale of intoxicants.

The weather was fine on Thursday, Friday and Saturday and each evening large crowds entered the fairground by the kindness of the Showmen's Guild, the takings from between 6 and 7 on the concluding evening was allocated to the Bridgwater hospital.

Chipperfield's Menagerie was crowded on Saturday night when Mrs Williams and Mrs Reeves of the Golden Ball Hotel, Bridgwater pluckily entered the cage of a lion. They entered separately and were accompanied by Mr Richard Chipperfield the menagerie trainer. Neither of the women showed fear. The lion gave the impression of being docile and showed compete indifference to the intrusion of strangers. During the short time the women were in the cage the trainer made the lions walk round the cage. Mrs Williams and Mrs Reeves were applauded for their pluck and presented with a box of chocolates."

In 1935 another ride that is still popular today made its debut at Bridgwater, the Waltzer, presented by well-known West Country showman, Tommy Whitelegg. Even at the start of the Waltzer's popularity in 1935 it was noted by reporters that the ride was made even faster by the attendants spinning the cars. In 1935 Whitelegg's Waltzer was joined by three Dodgem tracks and three Arks. Hill Bros also presented their Ghost Train for the first time. The Golden Dragons were now the Diving Dolphins and the Circuses of Chipperfield's and Paulo's were joined by Len Smith with his circus. featuring 'Big Chief Red Snake'. The cost of admission the Circus's was 6d for Chipperfield's and 2d for children and 4d for adults on the others. The shows include Sam Barton and Sullivan's Boxing Booths and Saxon Brown the Strong Man.

Above: One of Whitelegg's employees dressed as 'Charlie Chaplin' spinning the Waltzer cars. *[Whitelegg/Shepeard Collection]*

Charlie Heal was a popular Somerset Showman, born in Glastonbury, his business was based in Bristol. He was a generous benefactor to many good causes in the city. The firm even had its own football team.

In 1936 the headline in the local paper was the teasers and confetti had been banned once again by the council. The first ban was imposed at the instigation of the showmen in 1909 and had persisted for a few years. Teasers were water squirters and had been complained of for years and left the young ladies damp and dishevelled by the time they left the fair, if the rain had not already done so. The complainants were generally innocent bystanders squirted as a result of the intended victim ducking out of the way! The tradition of confetti throwing and the use of squirters went back at least a century before they were banned for the first time in 1909. The confetti and teasers (squirters) were merely an innocent, if crude device intended by young men to attract the attention of young women and engage them in conversation in an age when such situations were socially difficult to achieve. Billy Butlin who attended Bridgwater fair as travelling showman in the 1920s explained in his autobiography, *"In those days country fairs were the main meeting place for young men and women, and there was much larking about with boyish bravado and girlish giggles. The boys bought bags of*

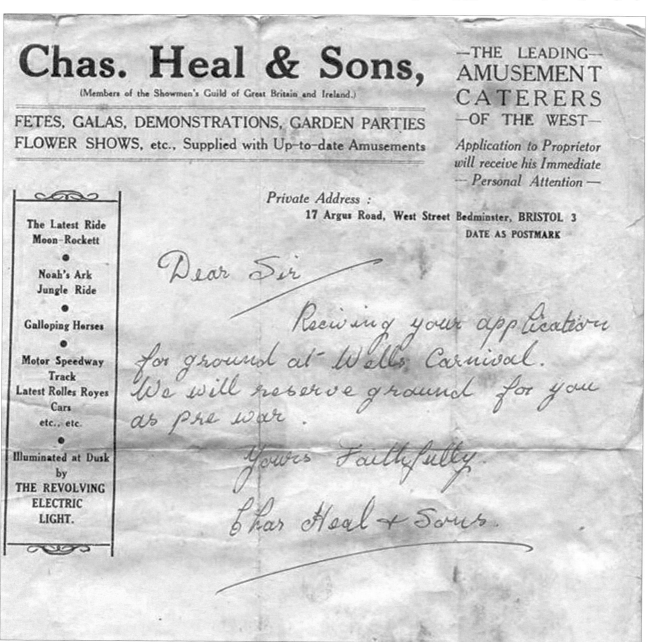

confetti at a halfpenny a time and threw it at any girl *that took his fancy. The girls retaliated with teasers, cylindrical containers made of soft lead with an opening like at the top of a toothpaste tube. You got two for a halfpenny and filled them with water and squirted them. Many a West Country marriage sprang from such pranks".*

A £32. 7/6 deposit was charged to Anderton & Rowlands in June for a deposit for their Dodgem and other attractions in 1934. The total paid for the rent for dodgems the Mont Blanc, small circus and 2 hooplas was £71.5s. The rides were much the same as the previous year and show included the Tattooed Lady, the African Fire Eater, the Midget Conjuror, Billy the Giant Pig, Nero the largest Dog, and a Wall of Death featuring a Lion riding on the wall. Three large refreshment marquees or beer tents were in operation until as recently as the early 1970s. Despite being a place to conduct business in a convivial atmosphere, occasional outbreaks of violence often involving gipsies or horse traders eventually resulted in these being abandoned.

By 1937, the coronation year, the fair had grown to be noticeably larger than ever, with the Bridgwater council collecting a record number of tolls from traders and showman with a record twelve adult rides and an ever

THEN THERE IS THE SECOND WONDER ATTRACTION: "NERO."

WORLD'S LARGEST ST. BERNARD DOG

Every man, woman, and child loves a dog, and here is the most gigantic, the most beautiful, and the most perfect specimen of the canine race the world has ever seen.

This beautiful animal is built on the proportions of a horse. His name is "Nero," and he is a St. Bernard, and his immense anatomy is a source of wonderment to dog lovers. He wears a collar over 3ft. long and eats between 25 to 35lb. of meat per day. He is as docile as a kitten, and children can ride on his back.

These Wonderful Animals are Valued at 10,000 Guineas

Above right: Nero-the largest dog. *Below:* Charles Heal Snr in the centre wearing a hat, Johnnie Heal and Charles Jnr with a member of staff in Mickey Mouse costume at the 1935 Fair, all the fittings on this popular machine, the Noah's Ark were chromium plated.

CORPORATION OF BRIDGWATER.

ST. MATTHEW'S FAIR — TOLLS. 161

Bigwood and Staple, Typ., Bridgwater.

June 30th 1934

Received of *Messrs* Anderton & Rowland. the sum of

Thirty two Pounds seven Shillings and six

Pence, being a deposit in respect of charges for ground for Roundabout

Dodgems &c

£ 32 : 7 : 6

W. Dunslade.

Collector.

Below: A magnificent line up with Anderton & Rowland's Scenic Railway and Jungle Ride starting the row of machines at Bridgwater Fair in the 1930s. *[Lionel Bathe, courtesy of the National Fairground Archive]*

MR. J. R. STYLES

growing number of smaller games and side shows. The more applications the council received from showmen and traders the larger the fair became. The *World's Fair* newspaper reported, *"this year's fair is much larger than any previous event. A great deal of praise is to be merited by the officials for the able way everything is presented. The ground that was previously an allotment has been fenced off and made solid. On Saturday evening, under the auspices of the Showman's Guild all proceeds from the rides from 8.00 and 9.00 pm was given over to the Bridgwater Hospital."*

The sensation of the fair that year was Tommy Whitelegg's Loch Ness Monster. A huge roundabout on which patrons sat facing outwards as the machine sped around a circular track at great speed.

The Monster was joined by the now familiar Dodgems, Noah's Arks and the Loop-o-Planes of Hill Bros, which took intrepid riders on a 360 degree loop the loop. Shows on offer in that year included an illusion show, the Headless Girl, the Bride of Frankenstein, the largest Schoolgirl, Chipperfield's Circus and Reaney's Coronation Circus, the Wall of Death and two Boxing booths.

One of the most well known showman to visit Bridgwater at this time was James Styles, who had his winter quarters at Bridge House, Bathpool near Taunton, but travelled far and wide with his shows. He did not own roundabouts or a circus but was indeed still a true 'showman' presenting a range of small but very smartly-presented novelty shows. Styles was a great orator, impeccably dressed and well spoken he would stand on the front of his show and draw the crowds in by his charismatic spieling. He is referred to in this report of the fair in the *World's Fair* in October 1933. At the fair that year he had his Palace of Varieties and Midget show: *"A great showman currently touring the West of England is Mr James Styles. There is no need to describe the outside of his Palace of Varieties for as long as such shows as his are on the road variety will never die. Mr Styles senior did the spieling himself with the aid of an amplifier and the way he spoke the King's English was a lesson even to a BBC announcer. I happened to be inside his show when one of the excise officers came round and asked everyone for their ticket. If ever there was an imposition then this entertainment tax is it, and all the novelty showmen should bring every available pressure to bear to endeavour to get this tax eliminated .After the show while chatting to Mr Styles he said the tax question was one of the evils that showmen must keep fighting."*

In 1938 gaps in the market traders in West Street were noted and it was the year of the 'war scare'. According to the press trade was reported to the worse for 18 years. By now the fair had been granted an extra day and was open on Saturday. The heavens opened that year and any chance of making up losses was dashed. The sheep entry was high with 7,000 sheep penned, although 1,500 down on 1937. The Market auction included 1,050 cheviots from Lord Fortescue. The entry of horses was very small with R.B Taylor & Sons offering just seven horses. The report in the *Mercury* painted a sombre picture: *"The fair opened with the war clouds hanging heavily over Europe, and every possibility that within a few hours England might be plunged into the terrible conflict. Visitors were not so numerous and did not enter into the spirit of fun with such gusto. A feature of the fair for some years now has been Chipperfield's Circus, in which the attractions included performing lions and bears. There was another circus of smaller dimensions. The many shows included the Wall of Death, Boxing Booth, the world's fattest married couple, the world's smallest women, the world's biggest schoolgirl, a native Prince with an unpronounceable name and striptease performance; Ladies in tents gazed in to crystals and foretold what the future had in store for their patrons. For one hour on Saturday the showmen gave their takings to the Bridgwater hospital."*

Anderton & Rowland's Dodgem, Ark and John Anderton's Children's ride, the Mono Railway were

Below: Members of the Whitelegg family and Hill families and staff on the new Monster ride. *[Whitelegg/Shepeard Collection]*

among the rides on offer. Jack Harvey presented the public with 'an amazing Scientific Mystery' the Headless Women and the Camel Horse and two Animal novelty shows comprised *Nero* the world's largest St. Bernard dog and *Dolly* and *Bobby* the racehorse twins.

The following report appeared in the *World's Fair* regarding the 1930 fair and refers to the strong tradition of Boxing Booths at the fair: *"Bridgwater loves a scrap–there were several private and personal affairs about the town, but the only official arena was Sam McKeowen's. Seeing the front empty, it is a new front and totally different to other academies, I thought the lads must be at their dinner. On my enquiry as to business, Mrs McKeowen smiled and drew the curtain, apologising as she did to the gentleman inside, they were literally standing on each others feet and even the door curtain could not be moved without disturbing the patrons who packed the house completely."*

The *Independent* Newspaper gives nearly half a column description of the boxers so they made some various impressions: *"Billy Taylor with a fistful of notes was throwing out challenges right and left."*

Billy Butlin in his autobiography recalls his acquaintance with Sam McKeowen during his time as a fairground showman in the West Country during the1920s: *"The Boxing Booth fighters challenged anyone in the crowd to go two or three rounds of three minutes with one of them for 10s of £1. Sam McKeowen*

SOMETHING ENTIRELY NEW FOR THE PUBLIC

All Lovers of Animals really must see the Aristocrats of the Animal World

"DOLLY AND BOBBY," THE TINY

RACEHORSE TWINS

Little "DOLLY" and little "BOBBY" are 24ins. high. They are the offspring of two ordinary size thoroughbred parents who are 16 and 16½ hands respectively. They are absolutely perfect in every detail, and are the true replica of their big brothers and sisters on the turf. It is about the only case in the world's history where thoroughbred racehorses have had twins, and it is almost impossible to recognise one from the other. They can jump like greyhounds. If you were to see them you would wonder how two ordinary size thoroughbreds could breed such minute horses; it is nothing less than marvellous.

THEY ARE JUST THE CUTEST LITTLE THINGS EVER BORN!

who ran the booth acted as both referee and time keeper. *This was a most useful combination for, if the challenger was a good scrapper, Sam would make the rounds a short three minute so that whether his man won (which he usually did because he was a pro) or lost he did so with the least of physical damage to himself. If there were no challengers one of the showman helped out by stepping up and pretending to be one of the public. They would put on a show, known as a 'gee fight' without hurting each other. Even I used to step up as a challenger, though Sam made sure I was matched against someone who was not too big or rough. Late at night you usually got some tough character full of beer and bravado looking for trouble. Those fights gave me useful experience you certainly had to look after yourself on the fairground."*

The Boxing booth has a long history on the fairground going back at least 200 years and took over from the bare knuckle bouts that were popular on fairgrounds prior to that Wrestling among locals was a popular sport across the west up until the middle of the 20th century. Elijah Lightwood, the lightweight champion of the West brought his booth to the fair in the 1860s. Lightwood was described in a contemporary report as *"a very respectable fellow and a great favourite with the followers of the prize ring. He always brought with him a first rate company of boxers."* Bridgwater usually had at least two booths and following the Second World War the booths stood at opposite ends of the show line at the bottom of the fair field. McKeowen's at the Horse and Jockey end and the West of England Boxing Academy presented at first by T. Whitelegg & Sons and later by Plymouth based Mickey Kiely.

The most famous booth boxer, Freddie Mills, the former milkman from Bournemouth joined Sam McKeowen's booth and appeared at Bridgwater between 1937 and 1939; after the fair he was called up to the armed forces. He joined the R.A.F. and became a corporal instructor and organised boxing tournaments for the R.A.F. Mills continued his fighting career and in June 1942 became Commonwealth and British Light Heavyweight Champion after defeating Len Harvey. The highlight of his career was in July 1948 when he became Light Heavyweight Champion of the World, beating Gus Lesnevich.

Mrs Esther McKeowen, the widow of the celebrated Sam, and her sons presented the last Booth to travel regularly in the West; she retired from exhibiting the

Below: Mickey Kiely's Boxing Show. *[Whitelegg/Shepeard Collection]*

PRESENTING THE FINEST BOXERS ON TOUR   TROUPE OF PROFESSIONAL CHALLENGING ALL COMERS

Above: Family members, showmen and staff in front of Kiely's Show. *[Whitelegg/Shepeard Collection]*

booth at the age of 93 and she died at the great age 101. Esther's husband Sam a well known Exeter-based showman was involved with the booth all of his life, as he was brought up by another west country booth promoter, Alf Wright. Alf Wright bought his booth to Bridgwater before the Great War.

Esther's parents, Jack and Alice Gratton, also ran a famous fairground boxing booth and Esther's brother Johnny 'One Round' Gratton was a well-known booth boxer and showman.   Esther had another brother, Tommy, also a keen boxer. Johnny Gratton attended Bridgwater fair all of his long life. He was a familiar figure with his cloth cap and rattle standing by the ball box of his coconut shy that he ran with his wife Selina (nee Whitelegg). He died in 1982 .

Many of the latest thrills were presented by Charles Heal and Sons. Mr. Heal was Bristol's most well-known showman and the first Charles Heal was from Glastonbury and the family claim the business was founded in 1881. They attended the fair from 1908 with their ornate 4-abreast Galloping Horse roundabout which appeared until it was sold in 1948. The Heal firm grew to such an extent that they operated two travelling

fairs after the war. They also had ride concessions on the Grand Pier at Weston Super Mare.

In 1940 they invested £2,600 on a new sensation, the Moonrocket, what is known in the fairground industry as a 'novelty'. This British built ride was manufactured by Robert J. Lakin of Streatham in London, one of most prolific producers of fairground rides at that time. The Moonrocket was a futuristic ride but is nearly always remembered for the figure of Popeye, seated on a rocket, which counter-rotated in the middle of the ride.

This demonstrates the success of this firm during a time of economic depression. Charles Heal senior died in 1950 and his son Albert took over the running of the fairground business.

The War Years

Above: Charles Heal's Noah's Ark, originally Hill Brothers and one of the few rides to open at Brdigwater in 1939 shorlty after the outbreak of war. *[New Era Library]*

On 3rd September 1939 Chamberlain's famous speech was broadcast to the nation at 11.15 a.m. announcing that *"this country is at war with Germany"*.

Arrangement for St Matthew's Fair had been made and deposits from those bringing attractions to the fair had been accepted. The *World's Fair* reported. The corporation displayed posters which read, *"St Matthew's Fair As Usual"*, but the pleasure fair was far from *"usual"*. There were only one Dodgem and an Ark in the way of big attractions. There were a number of side joints and houp-las and only two tents for the sale of intoxicants. But despite the depleted size of the fair large crowds turned out. The sheep sale went ahead as usual and the market was equally depleted. Owing to lighting restrictions the fair closed at sunset, about 7 o'clock. Glorious weather prevailed throughout and with brilliant moonlight each night conditions would have been ideal for the fair and the crowds would have been enormous in happier times.

The amusements in that year were Charles Heal's Dodgem and Hill Brothers' Noah's Ark. The latter was without rounding boards and had dark curtains rolled up under the tilt. Both rides were fitted with special dark coloured lamps. The only show was that of Lord Thomas Howard.

As part of the 'Dig for Victory Campaign' the part of the fair field usually used for the sheep fair was turned into allotments. By the summer of 1940 Somerset was plunged in to the full horror of attack by German bombers. The county suffered its first civilian casualties on 18th July when two people were killed by bombs dropped on Burnham on Sea. In August Bridgwater suffered seven deaths as the result of bombing on the night of Saturday 24/25th.

The fair was planned and took place as usual when many across the country were suspended for the duration. The age-old event must have been a great morale booster in those dark days of 1940 and after all it had an agricultural purpose as well as the pursuit of pleasure. The German action in targeting the supply lines of the shipping that brought in the country's food imports meant that rationing was in place and those that had made a living by making the fairings such as gingerbread and toffee and other confections were not able to do so for the duration and in many cases until sugar rationing was over.

In 1940 the emergency lighting restrictions meant the fair had to close at 7.30 p.m. but the report from the

World's Fair for that year indicated that the fair was still a great success: "*An ideal day as to weather, an ideal piece of ground on which the fair is held, even grass underfoot, a gathering of amusement quite up to what we must now call pre war level and a multitude of visitors seeking amusement and getting it. It was a surprisingly good collection of amusements and the responsive crowd seemed equally good. There was actually a brand new ride working and at capacity at this fair anyway. The centrepiece of the field, Charlie Heal's Moonrocket, was crowded for every run it made. I asked an old hand how many machines on the field? He answered five, but only one taking any money. The other rides were Heal's Dodgems, Anderton & Rowland's Dodgems and another Dodgem whose name escaped me as well as a Noah's Ark and Mono Rail. In the morning and afternoon they were all doing good business. These stalls as usual were old time throwing games, coconuts, touch-ems and darts. There was only one show this year Lord Thomas Howard's 'Giant Dog'. Again it was a lucky stroke and an unending stream of evacuated kiddies went in to inspect the canine breed. Out behind the amusement section into the cattle fair field through the many "hoss" dealers, did you ever see so many Romany chals together at once except at a funeral? Come past the long string of Exmoor ponies on past cobs hunters half-way hosse's even donkeys up to the sheep pens were 6,000 are in process of sale. Now look back towards the fair and say if you can that we English take our pleasures sadly. Not in Bridgwater! But no Nougat, no rock, no long strings of fruit stalls, no toffee making demonstrations- drat the sugar shortage!*"

Double daylight time was introduced in 1942 to maximise the hours of daylight which stretched opening hours without having to resort to black out covers. Rationing began that year, almost every commodity was affected from petrol and clothing to every type of food product as well as such luxuries as tobacco and alcohol. Sweet rationing hit the fair. No toffee, nougat, fudge or even toffee apples.

At the 1941 fair a ride that was to become the most well known at Bridgwater in the years after the war first appeared. Somerset showman Percy Cole bucked all the trends of the day and brought a Savage built steam-driven circular Switchback. Built in the 1880's and travelled by George Aspland of Boston. Known as the Venetian Gondolas, it later achieved a legendary status on the Steam Rally circuit. A report in the *Merry-go-*

Below: Heal's Moonrocket at Bridgwater. *[National Fairground Archive]*

Above: One of the rides for children at the 1940 Bridgwater Fair was a Monorail as shown in the view above, with a toyset to the left and shows, including Lord Thomas Howard's 'Giant Dog' in the background. *[Rod Fitzhugh]*
Below: Shows were much more popular in the days when the public saw less novelties via the television screen. The 'World's Smalles Man' was just one of the shows in the line at Bridgwater. *[Lionel Bathe, courtesy of the National Fairground Archive]*

Above: Charles Heal walking past Anderton & Rowland's Burrell *Earl Beatty* driving their Jungle Speedway which is to the left of Percy Cole's venetial Gondolas at Bridgwater Fair in 1941. *[DeVey Family]*

Round, a publication for fairground enthusiasts in the 1940s, reports on the machine's first appearance at Bridgwater: *"Mr. Percy Cole's Venetian Gondolas look like a brand new ride in perfect condition in every detail. The organ is a magnificent instrument very massive and looks like what it is, namely an ex-Bioscope show organ, still retaining much of the carved work and gilded figures. It plays splendidly and has a vast repertoire of music, both classical and popular. Mr Percy Cole is to be congratulated on his enterprise in acquiring and travelling this famous ride and in bringing it to a state of perfection. He richly deserves the splendid patronage which has been accorded it."*

These heavy machines were viewed as relics and several of the even more ornate Scenic such as the Golden Dragon type ride were bought up by Billy Butlin for around £500 a ride for his Holiday at Home programme.

The Gondolas were too big and cumbersome to travel in their original size, so in 1943, Mr Cole lowered the whole machine by two feet. It was still steam driven until 1956 when it appeared at Bridgwater driven by electricity and powered by a diesel generator. Some carved work was removed to lessen the load of travelling it, but despite these indignities to the grand old machine it still proved a magical glimpse in to the past to the many children taken on the ride with its twinkling bevelled mirrors and gilded carved work and tuneful organ. Percy Cole's Venetian Gondolas remained a firm favourite from after the war until their last appearance in 1976, when it moved to the Thursford Steam Collection in Norfolk where it remains to this day.

The china goods on offer as prizes on stalls in the fairground were in great demand by housewives in 1943 as there had been difficulty in obtaining crockery at Bridgwater and yet at the fair there were piles and piles on display. The *Mercury* reported. It would not be wide of the mark in saying that there was more china on display at the fair than could be found in the shops in the town. With the shortage that has been experienced people could but wonder where the abundance of china on the stalls came from. There were heaps of cups and saucers, plates, basins, dishes jugs, mugs and many other articles. To obtain any of the crockery visitors had to throw darts or engage in some other method. Iron and tin ware was in evidence and one visitor who was adept at dart throwing became the possessor of five kettles!

Above Percy Cole's Gondolas at Bridgwater with its original rounding boards. *[Lionel Bathe, courtesy of the National Fairground Archive] Below:* Putting on the Gondola cars. *[Rod Fitzhugh]*

Thrill seekers, at this the busiest fair since the war began, had a choice of Heal's Moonrocket, Cole's Gondolas, Gallopers, Speedway Ark, Chair-o-Planes and two Dodgems. There were three children's roundabouts, but alas, no toffee apples or nougat. The beer tent was absent due to a shortage of beer and no boxing booth, as the Mercury reported: *"The non existence of the booth was probably owing to members of the boxing fraternity fighting the enemy in various ways instead of pummelling one another in the ring. When will the Gingerbread be back? There were no coconuts to shy at but effigies including Hitler to hurl the balls at."* Shows included the Smallest Man in the World, The Living Pixie and Joy and Barney Worth (*below*) *"The World's Heaviest Married Couple"*, who posed with a sign saying, *"Look what rationing did for us!"* Two clairvoyants, one a man of colour, had tents inside the entrance to the ground. The amusement caterers arranged to give their takings from between four and five o'clock on Saturday to the Bridgwater Hospital. The total sum raised was £113.6s. The fair was the busiest the oldest residents could remember and the railways brought over 6,000 people in to the town.

As a consequence of more land being put under the plough sheep numbers were down. Altogether around 6,000 sheep were auctioned, which compared favourably with pre-war days, and the whole entry was cleared at reasonable prices. In the horse section a consignment of 20 Welsh ponies and foals attracted prices from 26 down to 8 guineas.

In 1944 with the cheerful expectation that it would be the last wartime fair, the crowd, according to the local press, were light hearted and intent on enjoying themselves and the old fair spirit was much in evidence. Crowds were even larger than the previous year and the showmen and traders of the town had a bonanza. Shooting galleries did a roaring trade and there were queues to get on the Dodgems. The fair had an international flavour as British Tommies and land girls mingled with many American G.I.s and Italian prisoners of war. There were very few stalls in West Street and those present offered yo-yos, flags and bunting. For the first time since 1938 the fair continued during the evening with the partial lifting of the blackout.

The rides on offer were as reported in the previous year with some new side shows, including *Flossie* the worlds smallest cow, 36 inches, Tarzan's lost Jungle, a two headed calf, an eight legged pig, the worlds largest rat ("*Hitler excluded,*" quipped the Mercury) and a Mickey Mouse Circus. A number of casualties were treated including several cases of fainting, some burns from a shooting range and a monkey bite, presumably from Tarzan's Jungle. Sheep numbers were down to 5,000 with a good entry of Dorset Downs, Exmoor and Cheviot breeds on offer by the Bridgwater Market Auctioneers and Taylor and Sons.

Post War Prosperity

Above: The Chair-o-Planes, Noah's Aks, Monorail and Moonrocket in the immediate post-war years, with a Rib Tickler or Mystic Swing in the foreground. *[Rod Fithugh]*

When life returned to normal in 1945-6 there was a huge demand for entertainment after the bleak dark black out days of the war. The fairground burst back into colour with the lifting of black out restrictions, the coloured lights blazed brighter than ever.

West Street Market was brimful of goods from home and abroad. Many long-rationed items were back in plentiful supply. St. Matthew's Fair 1945 was, of course, billed as 'The Victory Fair' with peace beginning on 9th May, but V.J. Day was celebrated in the month prior to the fair on 14th August.

For the 1945 fair the rides and stalls were bedecked with flags and bunting of the union flag along with those of the allies and was the biggest ever fair with many men from the fairground business that had served in the armed services returning to the fairs including George DeVey of Anderton and Rowland was one who attended while on leave from B.A.O.R.

The *World's Fair* describes St Matthew's Field as, "one seething mass of people from early morning until late at night" and indeed the fair enjoyed a bumper year. There were twelve large rides including Heal's Moonrocket, Cole's Gondolas, Chair-o-Planes, Gallopers, Dodgem and an Ark.

The *Mercury* reports the 1946 pleasure fair was *"Without doubt the biggest ever to come to Bridgwater.*

While the younger generation preferred the Moon Rocket, whirling around at 60 miles an hour, the older folk enjoyed themselves on the two sets of Galloping horses which revolved at a leisurely pace. The freak shows were well patronised as well, a pig with two tails; a calf with two heads; a living Sleeping Beauty; Tarzan's lost Jungle; The Living Pixie in his miniature house; the smallest cow and the house of a Million Laughs and of course there were the usual roll-em and darts. .People who expected to see a return of Coconut shies with real coconuts were disappointed-there were none! Servicemen, many of whom had not seen Bridgwater fair during war years , joined in the fun and it would not be surprising to know that hundreds of pounds that had been 'service' gratuities found their way into the coffers of the various stallholders and amusement caterers."

The years immediately after the war appear to have been the watershed for the fair, the shift from the emphasis from livestock mart to pleasure fair. Without doubt 1946 was the busiest fair for many years and possibly the best ever for the showmen. In 1946 there are claims from farmers and auctioneers that *"St Matthew's Fair is fast showing signs of becoming a Pleasure Fair"*. The number of horses and sheep was well down and bidding was anything but brisk. This could well have been a result of the way agriculture was starting to be influenced by government initiatives and directives concerning the centralization of cattle marts in general. New government agricultural policies after the war meant that a large number of fields previously grazed by sheep were put under the plough for the production of wheat. Mr.W.Giles, a local auctioneer, told the *Mercury* in 1947, *" We're turning the poor old country upside down–it's ploughing up here ploughing up there. That was never intended and if we go growing wheat we can't have livestock"* . The sheep entry was still 4,000 but well down on the pre war numbers of 6,000.

If the sheep sales were quiet then business was booming in West Street. The report from the *Mercury* in 1947 paints a scene of brisk trading in those halcyon days before the superstores supplied our every need: *"West Street was full of excited crowds jostling and pushing and screaming with delight. They exchanged remarks with stallholders and shouted with laughter at witty repartee. Everywhere the voices of salesman hoarsely shouting their wares. One only had to stop at a stall to be accosted and persuaded to buy. 'Can't you afford it?' disdainfully shouted one costermonger after anyone who resisted the temptation to buy. Cheapjacks vehemently declared themselves to me the most honest men on the earth. They had travelled to Bridgwater expressly to benefit the people of the town .They were quite happy to impoverish themselves to enrich their customers. It was only necessary to spend a small sum on a sealed envelope, raffle ticket or such like to become possessors of great wealth. The china stall on*

Below: Anderton & Rowland's new Swirl appeared at Bridgwater in the late 1940s and is seen next to Heal's Noah's Ark. Whitelegg's Dodgems and Waltzer can also be seen in this view, as well as some of the diesel tractors that hauled and generated for the rides. *[Lionel Bathe, courtesy of the National Fairground Archive]*

Penel Orliue was a wonderful sight. Coloured salad dishes in great variety and utility china sold swiftly. Women crowded around household stalls where everything from iron fenders to sealing wax was being loudly recommended by red faced men. The true Petticoat Lane touch was in evidence at the clothing stalls, where underwear suits and gowns were on sale and where coats where being forcibly tried on protesting women who had only come to look!"

In the fun fair new lighter faster rides were introduced in the post war days, the Dive-Bomber and the Jets reflected the public interest in air and space travel. Charles Heals and Sons' famous Moonrocket ride was introduced in 1939, after the war it was a firm favourite with teenage fair goers until the early 1960s. This was a huge circular ride, in which patrons sat in rocket styled cars. The illusion of even greater speed was achieved by having a large Popeye figure rotating in the opposite direction of the cars. It was a very heavy, labour intensive machine to transport and was eventually sold in 1962 and replaced by the Heals with lighter machines that were easier and less costly to erect and transport.

In 1947 the big attraction at the fair was the 'Sky Scraper', a Big Wheel that carried its passengers over sixty feet into the air, illuminated at dusk by thousands of fairy lamps, the glow of which could be seen for miles around the town. The Globe of Death also attracted thousands of people who saw remarkable displays of motorcycling at high speeds. Some members of the public had rides in the sidecar of one of the machines.

The following year the *Mercury* described the fun fair as *"The Million Pound Fun Fair". "The pleasure fair, valued at over a million pounds, was one of the largest ever assembled in any West Country town. Each evening the scores of sideshows and the twenty big rides dazzled in the glare of thousands of arc lamps. Sideshows included dancing girls, 'freaks' and singing mice".* Mrs Amy Lock was photographed on the front page above the caption. *"Born in a caravan 85 years ago. She says the fair at Bridgwater is the largest she can remember."*

With the pre war air of optimism and an embracing of all things American the rock'n'roll youth culture brought a new dimension to the fairgrounds. Music played at the fair mirrored the newly-established pop charts and became noticeably louder. The names of the rides were changed to embrace the new trends. The Noah's Ark or Jungle ride became the Speedway. Out went images of dance bands and classical imagery and in came rock and pop icons. Lighter rides that folded up and therefore easier to erect and dismantle and included many American designed machines such as the Eli-Bridge Big Wheel, Twist, Octopus, Dive Bomber, Meteorite and Rock-o-Plane.

The ever popular Dodgems, Arks and Waltzers remained and the show-line continued to prosper for the showman and arouse mirth and curiosity among the

Below: Line up of rides with Anderton & Rowland's Jungle Ride, Charles Heal's Ark and Roger's Speedway along with three sets of Dodgems and Albert Heal's Big Wheel. *[Blake Museum]*

Every year dozens of lorries bring the rides, shows and stalls for the fair. *Above:* The men load the platforms from Anderton & Rowland's Jungle Ride onto their Foden lorry *The Showman*. *Below:* One of the special Scammell 'Showtrac' lorries used by Anderton & Rowland: *Dragon* manoeuvres one of the big packing trucks into position. *[courtesy of the DeVey family]*

Above: Two of Tom Whitelegg's packing trucks stand in the street waiting to be collected by one of his diesal tractors and moved into position on West Street. *[Courtesy Ernie Taylor]* *Below:* Over the years showmen have used whatever vehicles werer available. Old buses were a firm favourite for many years. Here are two Bristol buses that have been converted into packing vehicles, standing at Bridgwater in the 1960s. *[DeVey family]*

public. Shows in the mid 1950's included the Reaney Family's Circus featuring 'Blitz' the educated pony, Barney and Joy the worlds heaviest married couple, combined weight 68 stones, Mr & Mrs Behrens the smallest married couple, Tiny Tim and his miniature motorcycle, Len Smith's Circus run by circus artists Denis and Zena Rosaire with *Simba* the five month old T.V lioness and their performing geese, Billy Watkins' freak shows, Shufflebottom's Wild West Show, Gratton's smallest horse in the world, Price's 'Belles of the Barbary Coast' strip show, Appleton Brothers' 'Show of Shows', Gary Whitehead's freak show as well as two boxing booths.

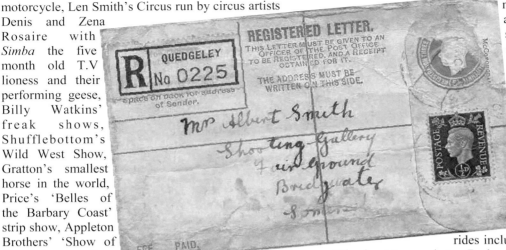

The 1949 fair was another hugely successful year for the fair and the *World's Fair* notes that the newer rides such as the Swirl and Dodgem were charging 3d a ride while the old favourites the Gondolas and Galloping Horses were riding at 6d.

The attractions were a typical post war mixture of boxing booths, strip shows, the Wild West Show, the Globe of Death, small circuses, the beer tents, the Waltzer and no less than five Dodgem tracks. On the last day the showman gave a percentage of their takings to local charities.

After the war the Western Showman's Social club was restarted under the chairmanship of Henry Charles. The subs of £1.10s. were collected at Bridgwater Fair. Activities included football and dances. An annual fair dance was an important part of the showfolk's social life at this time. At this time, veteran showman Jimmy Rowe organised parties for the children from the fair.

The *Independent* carried a charming photo of *Blitz* the Shetland pony *"with the human brain"* with its three day old colt *Lucky*. *Blitz* was star turn on Tom Reaney's Comedy Circus. The pony would tap out the correct answer to additions such as two plus two. A second image showed children standing around a lorry with *"real Live Teddy Bears"* painted across the back. These sun bears were presented by Exeter based showman, Gary Whitehead, and were features of the 1950 fair. Len Smith's show featured a popular visitor 'Big Chief Red Snake' and his 'Wonder Girls'. The little circus was described as *"a Hippodrome of Varieties."* These small circus shows held in a one pole tent featured ponies, clowns as well as acrobats and knife throwing acts.

The *Petticoat Lane of the West* tag was used by the *Independent* in its coverage of the West Street Market that year. China and linoleum were as popular as ever with a pet stall trading in goldfish and tortoises. One salesman was reported as giving away pound notes. Punters were asked to pay 6d for a sealed envelope, some of which, it was promised contained pound notes. This was a scam which later came to the attention of the police. A large china stall was pitched in Penel Orliue and stalls were erected on the Corn Hill during the 1950s.

In the coronation year of 1953 the rides included Charles Heal's Big Wheel, Moonrocket, Dodgems and Ark, Henry Chipperfield's Caterpillar, Percy Cole's Venetian Gondolas and Dodgem, T. Whitelegg & Sons' Waltzer and Speedway, Scottish showman William Codona's Waltzer, Alf Whitelegg's Gallopers, Sam Smart's Chair-o-Planes, Anderton & Rowland's Dodgem and Ark, Henry Rogers' and J. Whittingham's Ark and more Dodgems from Henry Rogers and Bernard Hill.

The *Mercury* described the scene at the busy fair in coronation year: *"The Big Wheel was the centre piece–a*

Above: Reaney's Circus brought *Blitz* the Pony with the Human Brain to Bridgwater. *[Lionel Bathe, courtesy of the National Fairground Archive]*

Above: A familiar sight at Brigwater Fair over the years, the Shooting Gallery. These often used live ammunition, but in recent years air-rifles have become mor usual. *Below:* Two sets of 4-abreast Galloping Horses, those of Charles Heal and Messrs. Anderton & Rowland, with Cole's Gondolas in the background. *Lionel Bathe, courtesy of the National Fairground Archive]*

Above: Percy Cole's famous Gondolas at bridgwater standing alongside William Codona's Waltzer, a stranger to the West, having travelled all the way from Scotland for the Coronation in 1953. *[Lional Bathe, courtesy of the National Fairground Archive.]*

revolving bracelet of twinkling light carrying its hordes of shrieking but happy people. The dodgems were doing a bumping business and the Helter Skelter attracted crowds, who polished the seats of their trousers with great enthusiasm. In a far corner of the field the Wild West Show was lassoing in the crowds who were eager to see naked bodies unflinching before thrown bowie knifes;scores lined up to see the world's smallest man, but a short distance away the fattest couple in the world were seeming to have a lean time. Next door a swarthy gent was shaving himself with a flaming brand! Boxing Booths were doing well .The fortune teller looked a little forlorn outside his tent. The Venetian Gondolas attracted the more sedate people and from under the hood of the caterpillar emanated shrieks of laughter. Above it all the music from the different shows blended in to one cacophony. Children wandered around with masses of pink candy flosses covering their faces and the licensed booths were packed to capacity.”

Sweet rationing came to an end in May of the coronation year so by the time of the fair the distribution system had built up ample supplies of all the old favourites and the sweet stalls in West Street were brim full of nougat, toffee and a dozen other sweets and colourful confections that the public had been denied the pleasure of for over a decade.

P.H. Becket was the Borough Treasurer responsible for allotting ground on the fair in the early 1950s. A civic opening was performed for the first time in 1954, the front page of the *World's Fair* shows a photo of the Mayor, Alderman A. Brindley-John, with members of the town council and prominent members of the Showmen's Guild, including chairman of the Western section Henry Rogers on the front of Reaney's Comedy Circus. The Mayor said the council was breaking new ground by opening the fair with a civic ceremony. It was hoped that in future occasions a civic opening might be carried out with picturesque ceremony and the attendance of the bellman and mace bearer in their uniforms. Tracing the ancient history of St. Matthew's Fair, he said it had been held at Bridgwater from time immemorial. The fair was held for eight days in the time of King John, who granted a charter for this period in 1200. King James I granted a charter in 1613 reducing the time for the fair to three days and in 1857 it was confirmed by a local act that the fair should be held on the last Wednesday in September.

Record crowds were once again reported in the local

press: *"The Mayor started a tradition that persists to this day by spending a few hectic minutes on the dodgems."* On the fairground two Bridgwater boys, aged 12, gave a boxing demonstration in the booth owned by Pat McKeowen. Frank and James Hogarth were the boys and their boxing described as 'fast and well timed'. Fine weather prevailed and the market did a good trade in lino, tea-sets and other household goods. Over 6,000 sheep were sold to a brisk trade as well as 60 ponies.

The *World's Fair* commented in 1956 that *"The most noticeable feature was the improvement to the entrance to the field. St. Matthews's Field has become in recent years an ideal ground for showmen; not like it was in the past, when potatoes were growing on the tober up to the Saturday prior to the Sunday pull-on."* There were twenty big rides that year including all the regular attendees plus Scottish showman William Codona. Shows included McKeowen's Boxing and Wrestling Show, Shufflebottom's Wild West, Reaney's Comedy Circus and Appleton's Glamour show.

The following year saw a larger fair with the return of a Wall of Death from Tommy Messham, Thomas Howard's Temple of Black Magic Show, Mickey Kiely adding another Boxing Booth and Billy Watkins' Freak show.

In 1958 showmen visiting the fair found the new Blake Road Bridge a great improvement in road conditions in the traffic clogged town. This second road bridge provided four carriageways. The sheep sales continued to hold up well during the decade and in 1958 3,200 sheep were penned. R.B Taylor and Sons reported a good selection of breeding and draft ewes, although good quality lambs were in short supply. Messrs. Tamlyn & Son reported a considerable improvement in sheep numbers at their auction at the fair's consignment of Cheviot ewes from Exmoor averaged £7 and W.H Palmer & Sons sold some good Chilver lambs from Mr. Morris of Thurloxton for a £9.2s per head.

The market in West Street was so crowded that reports talk of progress being reduced to a shuffle on fair day Wednesday 24th September. Fish and Chip Saloons and many confectionery stalls did a roaring trade, as did the beer tents and nearby Pubs.

Unusually the World's Fair published a complete list of tenants in the fairground, supplied from the town hall. Although mostly of interest to showman it is interesting to note that many of these same families are tenants at the fair in the 21st century.

Official List of Fair ground Tenants in 1958: F. Annear; Frank Austin; L.P Bennet; A. Biddall; J. Brewer; J. Brown; Reg Budd; George Butlin; J.A Butlin; Mrs A. Charles; T. Clements Senior & Jnr; Percy Cole Senior & P. Cole Jnr; C.F. Coneley, Marshall Coneley; Mrs M. Cooke; J.Da Costa; J.J. Edwards; J. Embling; G. Floyd Snr; G.F rankham; Johnny Gratton; Mrs E. Hamlin; Mrs

Above: Albert Smith, one of the old tenants who regularly attended Bridgwater Fair, seen here in the 1950s.

E. Harris; David Harrison, Johnny Harrison; Charles Heal, Joe Heal, Mrs L. Heal; Charlie Henderson; Marshall Hill Jnr, Bernard Hill, Mrs J. Hill; Arthur Hurrell, C.A. Hurrell; Tommy Hutchings; H. Jones, F.G. Jones; Andrew Keefe; A.H. Lennards; George Lock, M. F Lock; T. Manning; F. Mattia; R. McIntyre; S. McKeowen; J. Messham; R.T. Mott; Dennis Mutton, Leslie Mutton; W.G. Pocock; T. Pruett; Reg Rawlings, Jim Rawlings, L.J Rawlings; T. Reaney; George Rogers, Henry Rogers, Jack Rogers, Percy Rogers; Jimmy Rowe; Wm. Rowland, W. Rowland Jnr; Jim Saunders, Mrs L. Saunders; Henry Scarrott; William Shufflebottom; Jim Smart; Mrs. Alf Smith, Charlie Smith, George Smith; O. Smith, Tom Smith Snr; Mrs P. Stevens, R. Stevens; C. Stokes, J. Stokes Tom Stokes; H.A. Styles; E.M. Symonds, Mrs F. Symonds, G. Symonds; A. Turner; Bill Watkins; Charles Webb; Alfred Weston; D. Whitehead; A. Whitelegg, T. Whitelegg; C.S. Wynn; Anderton Bros; G. DeVey, N. DeVey; Wm. Codona; H. Guyatt; Professor Brown.

The attractions supplied by those in the above list were as diverse as shows called Dante's Inferno, Voodoo, Woman Alive, Beauty and the Beast, The Wild West

Above: Even Tiny Tim receives his post whilst at Bridgwater. *[Lionel Bathe, courtesy of the National Fairground Archive] Below:* Some of the last style of shows to appear at St. Matthew's Fair. *[DeVey family]*

Above: West Street Market before the demolition of the old terraces.

rights to open on that position in perpetuity, regardless of the nature of the piece of equipment operated. This well intentioned rule was intended to protect the rights of the smaller showman against his larger competitors, but critics see this as anti-competitive and ensuring that the same fair gets exactly the same rides and games every year with little place for new entrants to the business.

The fairground is one of the few businesses where one is either born or marries into it. For this reason a certain mystique has grown up around the business. The modern funfair industry is somewhat more prosaic than those outside would possibly imagine.

It is carried out within the same constraints and framework of rules and regulations as any other family business and the level of success or reward is generally, like all businesses, dependent on the amount of effort and investment made in it. It is a world of long hours continuous travel and wide fluctuations in income. Rather like agriculture, success or failure is dependent on the weather. There is a hierarchy among Guild members with those owning a number of rides at the top and those with side stalls and other games further down the scale. These operators of side joints and hooplas are generally the tenants of the machine owners at fairs. The machine owner who rents the fairground site from either a local council or private landowner is known as lessees

Show, a Freak animal show, Boxing Booths, The Wall of Death, as well as the rides typical of the decade the Rotor, Jets, Dive Bomber, Swirl, Dodgems and Big Wheel.

The last year of this turbulent decade on the world stage and in Bridgwater the pitchers and grafters returned to West Street to find the old familiar street changed for ever as many of the old houses and courts had been demolished and missing where the old familiar *"Parcels May Be Left Here"* signs. The old faces had returned with their familiar cries and wares the 'lino kings', 'crockery kings', run out merchants, hot dog sellers and second sight readers. In the fairground Testo's Flea Circus was a new novelty show and Gary Whitehead presented the curious Giraffe Necked Women.

"The Wettest Fair in Memory" was how the *Mercury* described the 1960 event, when *"rain of tropical intensity brought Bridgwater's historic St. Matthew's Fair to a premature conclusion shortly after 10.30 on Saturday night. Thousands rushed for shelter as the streets became awash and the fairground a sea of mud."* The showmen had to have their heavy loads and caravans pulled out of the field on the Monday following the fair and the field reduced to a quagmire.

In 1961 a significant change occurred: the running of the fair was taken over from Bridgwater Town council by the Western Section of the Showman's Guild, the organisation formed in part in 1889 by West Country showman and Bridgwater visitor Marshall Hill, among other notable showmen of the day, to protect the interest of travelling showmen. The Guild thereafter enforced their rules, the most contentious is a privilege to members known as the "two year rule". A showman occupying a position for two years has, in theory, the

Below: Testo's Flea Circus

BOROUGH OF BRIDGWATER.

Town Hall. Bridgwater.

P. H. BECKETT.
BOROUGH TREASURER.
REGISTRAR OF STOCK
AND
RATING & VALUATION OFFICER.

TEL: 2244/5

1 3 AUG 1952

Dear Sir/Madam,

St. Matthew's Fair, 1952.
24th - 27th September.

In reply to your application for space at the above Fair, ground has now been allocated to you as follows:-

Kind of Machine Show or Game	Measurements in feet			
	Frontage	Depth	Diameter	Area
Hoopla			14	

Your attention is drawn to the following points:

Turbines for the driving of riding machines will not be allowed in the centre of the ground but must be placed in the area provided, either on the South or North side of the Field.

All empty vehicles must be moved to the Cattle Market, Bath Road and will not be allowed to remain on the Field.

The possession of this letter authorises you to draw on to the ground. Living accommodation must be kept as close to the rear of the stalls as possible or alternatively in the South East corner of the Field. It is hoped by these measures to restrict living accommodation to persons genuinely booking ground.

Yours faithfully,

Borough Treasurer.

Above: Behind the side stalls is the community of showmen living in their wagon in the 1980s. *[Martin Burridge]*

and they set the rent to their tenants.

Children are educated partly by attending local schools and using learning distance packs and liasing with dedicated teachers and educational support staff when travelling. The children of travelling show people generally do as well academically as those from the settled community and many go through university to fulfil what ever vocational or professional ambitions they may have. Sons are often encouraged to take on the reins of the family business and many would never consider doing anything else. The show community is often seen as clannish, a notion perpetrated by the tradition of marrying into the business but this is by no means universal and many successful showman have married women from outside the business bringing fresh ideas and outlook on the business.

A person from outside the business is known as a "flattie". Thought to be derived from "flat earth". Not a completely derogatory term, simply a quick reference.

By necessity showmen live in caravans known as living wagons during the travelling season but it is not unusual for the family to also own a house and yard at their winter quarters.

Prior to the Showman's Guild administering the fair, tenants applied to the council for space and paid a deposit in June and the balance during the fair. When the Showmen's Guild took over they paid the council a sum for the total of the occupancy of St. Matthews's Field fairground and the council continued to collect individual tolls from the stall holders in West Street.

A contract is negotiated for, usually for a three year period, by the officials of the Guild and those of Sedgemoor District Council. The showmen appear to have little in the way of provision for their needs for the duration of the fair considering the amount paid over the years in rent. The travelling village that descends on St. Matthews's Field is temporary home to some fifty plus families plus their staff. The provision for electricity, water and sewerage disposal facilities appears to be inadequate compared to other famous fairground site and the excellent provision made on the continent. These are families that use the same facilities as the settled communities such as computers, TV's and the nature of the work means washing machines and tumble dryers are in constant use. These conditions however, have been improved in recent years. Other improvements to the ground include the provision of a road from the living wagon area on to the street that adjoins the field. The Guild collects tolls from individual showmen according to the class and size of the attraction.

The 1960s fair continued to reflect the changes in popular culture with music and lighting on the rides becoming more sophisticated as the decade progressed and rides such as the Octopus, Twist and the Trabant or Satellite appearing alongside the established machines. In 1961 the *Mercury* reported *"Record Breaking Crowds"* and glorious sunny weather, the fair was noted as *"the largest ever and included several new attractions. The big rides included the 60 year old steam roundabout , chair-o-planes, Big Wheel the hissing Jets, Dodgems, Waltzers, Lightning Swirl and new this year the Octopus and Calypso and the old time Helter Skelter had been renamed the Skylon."*

By way of a change in 1962 the *Mercury* decided to interview some of the showman at the fair. By contrast to the previous Indian summer the weather was appalling.

"Doyen of the fair was 82 year old Tom Smith. Tom, whose grandson and great grandson still appear at the fair, had only missed four fairs in his life and could remember when the first roundabout appeared. Another man born into the life was 69 year old Tom Reaney who has been coming to Bridgwater for 36 years. He used to run the little circus, but his family now present the Talk of the Town show. Born at St. Matthew's fair 42 years ago last Saturday was Pat McKeowen owner of one of the boxing booths. His father and grandfather owned the booth before him. For the story of how the fair used to be we talked to Ted Barrat, 72, who first came to St. Matthews field in 1892 when he was 12 months old."

The fair had a resident priest the Reverend Thomas Horne and a school in a tent for the children. The school mistress would travel with the show people. Along the show line Ghost Trains and Fun Houses began to replace some of the shows but the Boxing booths remained popular and Strip shows began to wane towards the end of the decade due to the more permissive attitudes that prevailed. The sheep and pony sales continued as part of the seemingly timeless agricultural calendar and agricultural implements were sold alongside the livestock.

The 1964 fair saw the debut of a new American novelty ride, the Twist. This was owned by Charles Heal and replaced the magnificent Moonrocket, a popular feature since 1940. From the operators point of

Below: Hill Brothers' Mont Blanc, Roger's Speedway, and Charles Heal's Noah's Ark are the first three rides in the line up at Bridgwater Fair in 194.. *[Lionel Bathe, courtesy of the National Fairground Archive]*

Above: John Gratton's Coconut Sheet in the late 1960's. *[Roger Evans] Below:* T. Whitelegg & Sons' Ghost Train.

view, much lighter and easier to erect and dismantle than the cumbersome Moonrocket. The fair in the early 1970s included John Lock's Ghost Train and McKeowen's Boxing booth. Ramon Henderson of the Showman's Guild described the fair as *"one of the largest ever seenat Bridgwater"*.

The new block of flats in West Street was finished in 1964 and stood like a Sentinel over the Fair. It was built by the Bridgwater Borough Council to replace the row of mid-Victorian terraced houses. It certainly seemed out of character in Somerset. The 1964 fair was the most successful since 1946 due to the Indian summer enjoyed that year. Beatles merchandise was much in evidence in the West Street Market, ranging from lapel badges, wigs, scrap books, and even blankets. Good weather continued to prevail at the fair the following year and the fair was featured on the television for the first time.

Up to 50,000 people were reported to have visited the1965 fair on the final day.

The *Mercury* heralded the 1966 fair with the claim the headline, *"Fair could be a Record Breaker, £2 Million Pound Amusement Park. The Showmen were hoping for a bumper year due the recent opening of the Severn Bridge. Indeed the crowd s were described as 'record'.* And the fair was blessed with fine dry sunny weather for the duration. However Albert Heal chairman of the Showman's Guild reported that money was not spent freely and the showman had experienced one of the worst Thursdays they could remember. *'Business was very bad,'* said Mr. Heal, *'but you don't expect much during the week these days'."*

Over 6,000 sheep and115 horse were for sale and the Mayor, Alderman E.J Davies, made an official visit to the fair, the first time for many years. An interesting feature was included in the *Mercury's* report included an interview with two old timers on the fair, 86 year-old Tom Smith and 68 year old Charles Coneley. Tom remembered that a Mr Denman was the lessee of the fair in the 1880's. Sitting on a bench near the West Street entrance to the fair Tom Smith told the reporter: *"I've* seen the mud so deep here that the wagons sunk in and that's were we left them and carried the stuff in. It was not laid out like it was now. In those days there used to be a lot of 'gippos' and horse dealers and more business was done. The fair partly pulled down on the Thursday night and we'd go on stopping at Shipham and Bedminster Down to rest the hosses and open at Gloucester on the Saturday. I came here once with old Charley Wynn, .Gosh that was a night! They nearly set alight to the hooplas with squibs. I said never no more will I come here. But mind 'twas a good procession. But there weren't many hooplas here in my early days. There was old Mrs Betty's Cake Stall and cockles and a wild beast show, Chipperfields, no sound but dancing girls in front of the show. and there was conjuring and knife throwing. Dickie Dooner had the picture show, but Albany Wards killed that off. I used to have Coconut shies and a striker where they had to hit the bell. And Billy Butlin used to be here with a lot of stuff."

Charles Coneley told the *Mercury's* man, *"I'm 68 and been here all my life and father before me. Very small fair it used to be, two set of Horses and two Switchbacks and Hancock's and Anderton's Living Picture shows. The fair is more than ten times the size it used to be and there are show people from the Midlands and London,* they only used to come from the west country...They've got better equipment and better organised."

The 1970s was the swansong for the live shows, the Boxing booths found it harder to attract willing participants and Mr Shufflebottom, the famous Wild West knife thrower, hung up his axes and knives towards the middle of the decade. Strip shows ceased to appear around the same time; Tommy Messham's Wall of Death roared around for the last time in 1982. The Wall hit the headlines in 1979 when a Russian rider collided with the proprietor and suffered a broken shoulder.

A major news story in 1971 in the *Mercury* and indeed on local television centred on 45 year-old roundabout owner Alfie Whitelegg and the loss of his position for his famous Galloping Horse roundabout at the fair following a family dispute. Alfie's father died in 1969 and left the roundabout to his sons and daughters but left a condition in his will that if they could not agree to work together the Gallopers were to be put up for public auction. Alfie bought the famous machine for £11,500 but the position at St Matthew's and Barnstaple Fair were sold separately to his two brothers. Alfie told the *Mercury* in August 1971: *"I had a chance to buy the sites myself, but I thought as I was carrying on my*

Below: Alfie and Tom Whitelegg building up the Gallopers. *[Gloria Westley]*

Above: A quiet afternoon at Bridgwater Fair, showing the Chair-o-Planes, with Anderton Brothers' Toytown children's ride to the left behind the round-stall. To the immediate left of the Chair-o-Planes is a Buzz-Bomb ride, a children's roundabout constructed after the war using the fuel tanks from Second World War aircraft. These were all popular attractions at Bridgwater for many years. The image also shows some of the side stalls which build up around the edge of the ground, offering opportunities to win on games such as darts, guns, roll-down tables or other throwing games. Behind these are some of the lorries and living wagons which all make up the fairground. *[Lionel Bathe, courtesy of the National Fairground Archive]*

Above: 1950s Glamour Show *[DeVey family]* *Below:* Alf Whitelegg's Gallopers and Cole's Gondolas.

father's business in his name, the sites would automatically be mine. I have offered my brothers £400 for one site alone but they just aren't selling. I have appealed to the Showman's Guild to see if they can get me my sites back. If they can't help I don't know what I shall do or where I will go."

There was a scathing comment on the behaviour of the Showmen's Guild by a very sympathetic *Mercury* in its coverage of the fair that year under a head line, *"The Gallopers were non-starters...Fair wasn't the same without them...Bridgwater Fair was minus one of its most important ingredients. The public had been deprived of rides on Alfie Whitelegg's Golden Gallopers. And the agony of it all was that the Gallopers were at the fair...but inside a massive wagon that Alfie couldn't unload because of a ruling made by the Showman's Guild in London. How this came about is too complicated to go into here, but let us hope that next year Alfie will be back in that corner of the field where we have always known to find him. Most definitely none of the modern machines compensated for their absence, which became a topic of conversation from one end of town to the other. It must never happen again, Showmen's Guild please take note. Bridgwater folk are quick to forgive but deprivation of something they really love and look forward to such as those Gallopers is akin to forbidding the carnival procession. I myself am not at*

all sure that everything that could be done was done to ensure Alfie Whitelegg was accommodated in the fair field." Eventually Whitelegg did regain a position at the fair for his famous roundabout but on a less prominent position.

The show line that contained such an intriguing, colourful and bizarre rosta of attractions during the past centuries was given over to the more prosaic slots arcades, bouncy castles and funhouses. Live entertainment, for so long an integral and popular part of Bridgwater fair was gone forever. Many fair goers considered this to be a great shame and the fair did lose a little of its character. The fondest and most vivid memories of many older residents of the town are of the shows. The shows disappeared but the term *showman* is still the preferred way to describe an operator of fairground equipment. Many of the small circus shows performed in the one pole tent behind a walk up façade were a quaint mixture of displays of equestrian prowess, conjuring, acrobatics and clowning and were run by closely knit family companies made up of hard working performers for little financial reward and offered good value for money entertainment Other novelty shows were ingenious and charming while just a few were quite reprehensible and unsavoury.

Above: Drumming up business on the front of the Boxing Booth in the early 1970's *[Roger Evans] Below:* Anderton & Rowland*'s* Noah's Ark with Ernie DeVey and staff at Bridgwater after fitting scooters. *[DeVey family]*

Above: Esther McKeowen with her sons Pat and Bernard in the 1970s. *[Martin Burridge]* *Below:* The mayor of Bridgwater enjoying Heal's Dodgems following the civic opening of the fair. *[Billy Whitelegg]*

During the 1970s the rides remained little changed since the previous decade and the Noah's Ark that began life before the war decorated with jungle scenery and exotic carved animals such as monkeys and giraffes having been transformed to the motorcycle Speedway in the 1950s now became revolving discothèques known as the Disco Ark and Psychedelic Speedway with ultra violet light, powerful strobes and flashing lights pulsating to the popular music of the day. The teenage punters found the biggest thrill in trying to stand on the platform for as long as possible as the thing sped around faster and faster. The greasy looking *gaff lads*, the casual labour employed by the showmen, leaned nonchalantly chewing gum, standing at just the right angle. To impress the girls they would hop off the speeding platform to the central paybox and back on again as if hopping off the bus.

The street market remained as popular as ever with a cornucopia of goods on offer from bulbs for the garden to crockery, fashion ware and confectionery. The street market remains an important part of the fair to this day. West Street is the former site of the sheep market until it was redeveloped in the 1950s. and further still at the end of the 1960s.

The opening of the M5 Motorway in 1972 relieved the town of the daily blight of traffic congestion and made travelling to the town much easier for the showman.

Above: Mrs Fay Clements and her sisters, long-standing tenants at Bridgwater Fair. *[Martin Burridge]*

In 1974 the large scale changes in local government saw the end of the Bridgwater Borough Council the Bridgwater Rural District Council and Burnham on Sea Council, all of which were replace by Sedgemoor District Council which was responsible for the operating of St. Matthew's Fair.

The 1980s saw a little in the way of innovation on the fairground as new larger continental rides started to appear but the Dodgems, Big Wheels and Waltzers continued to be as popular as they had for the past fifty years or so. The Noah's Ark began to disappear as a consequence of far tighter safety rules that forbids riders from standing during the ride.

The last decade in the 20th century saw many new innovations on the fairground. The amusement industry in Germany and Italy has raced ahead of its British counterpart since the war and the 1990's saw the fair starting to bring in a selection of continental innovations such as the Top Spin, Enterprise, Matterhorn, Sea Storm and since the dawn of the new century huge attractions the Top Buzz, Chaos and the spectacular Wild Mouse Spinning Roller Coaster.

The sheep sales ended in 2001 following new regulations following the foot and mouth disease outbreak, but the unofficial horse sales continue and the fair day market is held on the site of the former sheep pens.

Today the running of St. Matthew's Fair, the West Street and Fair Field market along with the fun fair are the responsibility of Sedgemoor District Councils Markets and Fairs Department. The overall planning and running of the event are managed by Martin Roberts, the district valuer and his team. Martin works closely with the Showmen's Guild and the National Federation of Market Traders. These two trade organisations represent all tenants at the event, both in the market and on the fairground. There are 100 stalls in West Street and, generally speaking, the same tenants return to the same pitch each year. A recent innovation, following complaints from residents, is the provision by the council of silent running generators for use by the traders in West Street.

The organising of the fair involves liaising with the Fire Service and the Police who are responsible for traffic management and policing the market and fairground. The council has a site office.

The Showmen's Guild is responsible for allotting ground to regular and new tenants, setting out the ground in agreement with the council, arbitrating disputes between members and the marketing of the fair by means of TV advertising, placing posters and generating any publicity with the local media. The main factor between successes or failure, the weather, in the hands of a higher authority, than even the Sedgemoor

District Council or the Showmen's Guild.

Tom King M.P, for many years the member for the large constituency of Bridgwater. Mr. King always took a keen interest in the Fair. His position as Northern Ireland Minister sometimes gave his security personnel some headaches, such as this trip through the Ghost Train in 1998.

St Matthew's Fair is still largely on 'fair day' a family occasion and the towering thrill rides sit cheek by jowl with the Noyce's beautiful Galloping Horses and the plethora of children's roundabouts that go to make sure the event appeals to all ages.

Although the thrill rides have become bigger, faster and more sophisticated and the shows have sadly disappeared, the inherent atmosphere of Bridgwater fair remains. A sense of unchanging tradition in a splendid semi rural setting, with the Quantock hills in the background.

If fine weather prevails, St Matthew's Fair on fair day offers a unique day out with a great sense of continuity and tradition. The scent of mud and trodden grass, ponies being led around by gipsy lads, the pomp of the Mayor opening the fair, school children afforded a day

off amid the rumble of the fairground generators and the cry of barkers. Horses are still traded; coconuts are still shied for and children still ride on gilded Galloping Horse roundabouts and slide down Helter Skelters as generations of children have done. And the day is still rounded with a treat of those sticky confections forever associated with the fair: Candy Floss and Toffee Apples.

Teenagers still gather on the steps of the Waltzer and Dodgems and continuity is preserved by the same show families providing entertainment as their ancestors did in the 19th century.

These families started with shows and steam roundabouts and have progressed through the 20th century and in to the 21st with the latest attractions, always "First with the Latest"!

Below: Tom King M.P. on the Ghost Train at Bridgwater. *[Guy Belshaw]*

Acknowledgements

I would like to thanks the following people without whose help and support this book would not have been possible: Dr Vanessa Toulmin, Ian Trowell and Tim Neal of the National Fairground Archive at Sheffield University; the Bridgwater Mercury; Rod Fitzhugh; Roger Evans; Ernie Taylor, Martin Burridge; Stephen Smith; Kevin Scrivens; the DeVey family; Billy Whitelegg; Rosie Small; Gloria Westley; Martin Roberts (Sedgemoor District Council); John Cole; Dave Hartley (proof reading); the staff at the Somerset Studies Library, Taunton Main Library; the Western Section of the Showmen's Guild of Great Britain and my wife, Alison.